So You Wanna Read Tarot?

A Down-to-Earth Guide

D. L. Cocchio

©2012

Copyright © 2012 D. L. Cocchio

All rights reserved. No part of this book may be reproduced in any form without written permission from the publishers, except by a reviewer who may quote brief passages in a review to be printed in a newspaper, or magazine.

Illustrations from the Rider-Waite Tarot Deck®, known also as the Rider Tarot and the Waite Tarot, reproduced by permission of U.S. Games Systems, Inc., Stamford, CT 06902 USA. Copyright ©1971 by U.S. Games Systems, Inc. Further reproduction prohibited. The Rider-Waite Tarot Deck® is a registered trademark of U.S. Games Systems, Inc.

Front cover photography commissioned by D. L. Cocchio from *4 Cats & A Baby Photography* –
Leann Cook Knowles, photographer.
Cover model - Jennifer Cocchio.

Permissions to use The Rider Tarot card images on the cover were also granted by U.S. Games Systems, Inc. - credits shown above.

Additional interior photos purchased through fotolia.com, istockphoto.com, and dreamstime.com.
Public domain clipart from Microsoft Office.

ISBN-10: 0615514715
ISBN-13: 978-0615514710
First Printing March 2012.
Published by Magic Moon Press.
Printed in the United States of America.

Dedication

To my family and friends -

You've been my encouragement

and support through this

whole enlightenment.

I love you all!

Acknowledgements

With special thanks:

~ to my husband, Gary, for his unwavering support and faith in me.

~ to my daughter, Jen, for allowing me to teach her the tarot as I wrote this manuscript. And for graciously agreeing to model for the cover.

~to my tarot buddy, Debbie Campoli, for being my beta reader and for generously sharing her honest critique and suggestions. And mostly for being such a great friend!

~ to all my tarot students for encouraging me to put it all in writing.

~ to my guides for their steady guidance.

~ and to my friends and family, who always believed in my success.

TABLE OF CONTENTS

1. Welcome to the World of Tarot! 3
2. How Do They Do It? 5
3. Choosing Your Own Deck 9
4. Creating Your Own Space 19
5. Where Did It All Start? 25
6. Look A Bit Closer 31
7. Major Arcana 37
8. The Suits 107
9. The King and His Court 113
10. Minor Arcana 123
11. Reading Reversed Cards 131
12. Astrology Fun 137
13. Are You Ready? 145
14. Shuffle Those Cards 149
15. Think Before You Speak 157
16. Can We Play Games? 163

17. Popular Tarot Spreads — 169
18. The Cheat Sheets — 189
19. Completion — 201

Chapter 1

Welcome to the World of Tarot!

If you are reading these words, then you are curious about the Tarot Cards and want to learn more. I truly believe that there is a reason for everything that happens in this world and really believe in the saying, "When the student is ready, the teacher appears". Well, *welcome to the class*. I plan on helping you discover a whole new world as you uncover the true meaning of each tarot card. You'll eventually learn every symbol, every suit, every color and every meaning without even realizing you've done it.

Once you begin to learn Tarot you will acquire a "thirst" for knowledge. You'll want to know more and more. I can't tell you how many Tarot books I've read over the years. Many of them were so esoteric (understood by only a chosen few), that it was hard getting past the language to understand what the author really meant to say. So, I decided to write this very basic, beginner book on reading Tarot Cards, using down-to-earth language and

D. L. Cocchio

descriptions. I tried to make it easy to understand so that teenagers and beginners could find the information that they need to get started in Tarot without being turned off too easily by complicated language. This book can also be a useful tool for tarot readers who want to brush up on their skills.

I wrote this book for my daughter Jen, who was in her teens when I wrote it. Through my descriptions, tips, games and illustrations, she has learned the plain and simple meanings of the Tarot cards, just like you will.

After reading this book you will be able to do some fun readings for your friends, be the life of the party, or just get to know yourself better through your own tarot readings.

Good Luck and Happy Tarot Readings!

D. L. Cocchio

Chapter 2

How Do They Do It?

Many people can't explain just how the Tarot Cards work or how readers get their information. It is common belief that the Tarot Cards are simply a tool to help you focus. The Tarot is like having pieces to a puzzle and you, as the reader, get to put the puzzle together to make some sense of it. Outside forces such as your spirit guides, the angels, God, and your higher self are all able to communicate by showing you the answers in symbol form. Since our minds think in symbols, it's only logical that these cards, which tell stories through symbols, could help our intuition. You just have to quiet yourself and listen. The symbols will be discussed further, later on in this book.

Some people have the wrong attitude about readers. The rumors say that most readers come out with general statements that could mean something to just about everyone. Perhaps, the ones that are making the accusations had a terrible reading by an unskilled reader at one time, thus influencing their opinion of readers in general. Unfortunately, these types of dishonest readers give the rest of us a bad name.

"It gives the rest of us a bad name."

It's true that some people are in it for the money. I've seen some boardwalk fortune-tellers that also give the rest of us a bad name by telling fortunes that are general and could apply to just about anyone. Then they go on to tell you that they could tell you much, much more for an additional fee or they say they can rid you of an evil curse that you have on you for a mere $500.00.

Yeah, right!

*Just trust your intuition
and **run** if this happens!*

But, the majority of tarot readers are sincere and truly can help to give direction and meaning to our lives.

 Try This:

Meditate On a Card

Look through the cards and choose one that you like and are drawn to. Sit in a place that is quiet and study the card, and then meditate quietly about it. Clear your mind and see what thoughts pop into your head about this card. Jot it down in your journal. Look at the picture and make up a story about what you think is going on in the scene. Jot down some notes about what you envision. This helps you to develop your intuition and your meditating skills. Eventually you will learn to trust your intuition or your gut feeling.

D. L. Cocchio

Rider-Waite Tarot Cards

Chapter 3

Choosing Your Deck

Which deck screams "Choose me!" The most important thing to remember is to choose a deck that you feel comfortable with. It has been rumored that a deck should be given to you as a gift. This is good, but not necessary. It is just an old wives' tale.

In this book I will be describing the Rider-Waite Tarot Card deck, also known as The Rider Tarot, which is a great one to begin with. The Rider-Waite deck is very basic and is full of symbols. The pictures are very precise and clear, giving inspiration to your intuition. The illustrations are easy to comprehend and are not complicated by too much action. Many tarot decks are fashioned after this one. I suggest you start with the Rider-Waite deck. If the colors are too bright for your liking, The Universal Waite Deck is essentially the same deck, only it is painted in pastel colors. The paintings are a little more muted. You may find that you like this deck better. *I know, I do.* The Universal Waite Tarot Deck has drawings by Pamela Coleman Smith, coloring by Mary Hanson-Roberts, and was conceived by Stuart R. Kaplan. When you get confident in your ability, you can graduate to a deck of your choosing. Once you learn the Rider-Waite or Universal Waite decks, you'll be able to read most of the decks that you pick up. Most of them share universal symbols to represent the common events that happen in life.

"Choose a deck that speaks to you."

When choosing a personal deck (after learning), ask yourself which cards appeal to you? Sometimes the deck chooses you. Choose a deck that "speaks" to you; one that has pictures or subjects that you are interested in and things that catch your attention. That's what I mean by a deck that speaks to you. Some readers like to have two different decks for variety. Most stores have them on display so that you can thumb through the whole deck. Do this so that you can get a feel for what is right for you. Some decks have a card called "Transition" instead of the traditional "Devil". This is less threatening to some readers and makes their friends and clients more at ease. It depends on what you like. Both cards have the same exact meaning.

I think that I must have about two dozen decks to play with. It depends on what mood I am in as to which one I use. But, you may turn out to be a one-deck reader.

Remember to choose a deck that appeals to your sense of color, style, and imagery, contains visual appeal and stimulates your imagination. Some other popular tarot decks to consider are:

Some Classic Tarot Decks

The Rider-Waite Tarot (or Rider Tarot) - The most widely used of all Tarot decks. Many other decks have been fashioned after this one. It is influenced by the Hermetic Order of the Golden Dawn and known for its clear symbols. The Rider-Waite was conceived by A.E. White and designed by Pamela Colman Smith.

The Universal Waite Tarot - A deck created in 1916 by Arthur Waite, a 20th century occultist. It is very similar to the Rider-Waite with pastel colorings and is based on drawings by Pamela Colman Smith and the colorings by Mary Hanson-Roberts. The deck was conceived by Stuart R. Kaplan.

The Golden Dawn Tarot – This deck was painted by Robert Wang with Dr. Israel Regardi and based on the interpretations of S.L. MacGregor Mathers. It incorporates astrology, the elements, planets, and the zodiac.

The Thoth Deck – Created by Aleister Crowley and an artist named Lady Frieda Harris. Crowley was a noted occultist and magician in 20th century England. The designs contain astrological and Kabbalistic symbols.

The Hanson-Roberts Deck – Mary Hanson-Roberts illustrated this deck with fairytale-like illustrations of the Rider-Waite style.

The Connolly Tarot – This deck was created by Eileen and Peter Connolly with spiritual imagery and is simple and clear in their message. There is no Death Card, instead a card called Transition. Also, the Devil card has been re-titled Transformation.

Zolar's Astrological Tarot – These color-coded tarot cards are based on the Rider-Waite deck and contain interpretations written right on the card.

The Morgan Greer Deck – It boasts beautifully illustrated borderless pictures drawn with the Rider-Waite pack in mind. The figures are more whimsical and animated. It was created by Bill F. Greer and Lloyd Morgan, based on interpretations of Paul Foster Case and Arthur Edward Waite.

Next is a listing of specialty tarot decks that you might consider:

Goddesses and Mythology

Celtic Tarot – It combines Celtic art and myths with the wisdom of the ages by Courtney Davis.

Arthurian Tarot – These cards display all of the wonder and beauty of King Arthur's realm, by Caitlin and John Matthews and painted by Miranda Gray.

Merlin Tarot – This deck shows images, insight and wisdom from the time of Merlin, by R.J. Stewart and illustrated by Miranda Gray.

Medicine Woman Tarot – It incorporates sacred Native American images honoring Mother Earth, by Carol Bridges.

Fantasy Tarot Decks

Wonderland Tarot – These cards are based on "Alice in Wonderland" type drawings, designed by Christopher and Morgana Abbey.

Lord of the Rings Tarot – It is based on the "Lord of the Rings" book written by J. R. Tolkien.

Tarot of the Cat People – A deck with unique feline illustrations incorporated into the pictures by Karen Kuykendall.

Historical Tarot Decks

Visconti-Sforza Deck – A beautiful deck from Italy that originated in the 15th century with old world charm by Bembo.

Classic Tarot – This deck has classic Italian drawings as illustrations by Stuart R. Kaplan.

Tarot de Marseilles – It is a fantastic reproduction of a 1760 deck from Marseilles.

Medieval Scapini Tarot – This deck contains illustrations from the Renaissance and Middle Ages by Luigi Scapini.

Spiritual Tarot Decks

Tarot of the Old Path – Howard Rodway designed this deck with the assistance of a coven of 8 witches. It contains pastel mystical illustrations of the old religion.

Tarot of the Sacred Rose – A deck done in stained glass pictures with red and black undertones by Johanna Sherman.

The Lover's Tarot – These cards will answer all questions on affairs of the heart by Jane Lyle.

Herbal Tarot – Each card in this deck shows a different herb for their healing powers by Michael Tierra and Candis Cantin.

Tarot of the Witches – These cards contain paintings by Fergus Hall of dream-like fantasies.

International Tarot Cards

1JJ Swiss Tarot – A deck that originates from the 17th century that incorporates some mythology by R. Kaplan.

Japanese Tarot – Japanese figures in historical costumes with traditional Japanese symbolism are in this deck.

Egyptian Tarot Deck – Comte C. de Saint-Germaine based this deck on Egyptian mythology and culture.

Chinese Tarot – The imagery in this deck combines symbols, legends, beliefs, and customs of Ancient China by Yury Shakov.

Russian Tarot of St. Petersburg – The illustrations on these cards depict Russian folk and fairy tales.

Norse Tarot – Clive Barrett combines Viking imagery with the Tarot in this deck.

Note: Many of these decks are available through U.S. Games Systems, Stamford, CT. or through your local New Age Bookstore.

Hint: You can look them up online by searching on *Google* to see photos of the cards' illustrations and decide if they resonate with you or you can see them in-person at your local new-age bookstore.

Deck Care:

Many readers believe that the cards should be wrapped in a piece of silk so that their energy does not weaken. Another good suggestion is to store them in a silk bag or a wooden box for protection. Wood is supposed to protect against negative influences. A silk scarf works just as well for protection when you use it to wrap your cards. If you decide to make a bag yourself, it adds your vibrations to it. This is not necessary, but a nice touch. A store bought bag can also serve the purpose. Inside the bag I keep a small quartz crystal for clarity and a cross to help me feel protected. Store the cards whichever way feels right to you and with whatever stones or trinkets that make you feel secure. Trust your intuition.

It is important to handle your cards as often as you can so they can absorb your vibrations. Try to remember not to handle them when you are upset or in a bad mood, because they will soak up those bad vibrations as well. It is good to occasionally cleanse your cards and clear away any negativity by passing them through the smoke when you burn incense or sage. Some readers have a thing about people touching their cards, but many like to have the person they will be reading for shuffle the deck while thinking about the subject at hand. It adds their vibrations to the reading. Everyone is different. You'll decide what is right and which works best for you. Personally, I prefer to let my clients shuffle the deck.

"Wrap your cards in silk."

It has also been recommended to sleep with the cards under your pillow in order to learn them. You can try this too, but many have found that you just wake up with the cards all over the place in the morning. If you want to try this, a suggestion would be one card at a time, perhaps meditating on that card as you fall asleep. When you wake in the morning, jot down notes in a journal about what you remember about the card. This will help you later on. It is also helpful to keep this new journal with you when you are learning the cards, so it is handy for taking notes along the way. You can refer to these notes often to aid in your interpretation of the cards.

 **Try This:**

Decorate Your Own Tarot Box or Bag

You can find a bag or a box at a New Age shop near you or you can make one yourself. For instance, you could make a tarot box out of an old cigar box that Dad or Grandpa might have. Cigar stores sometimes sell empty boxes. Some of them are wooden too. You can cover it in fabric or felt if you like, or even adorn it with buttons, magazine photos, stones, or trinkets. If you store some incense in the box for a few days, the cigar scent will disappear. Another idea is that you can use a fancy cloth bag left over from perfume and decorate it with beads if you like. Let your imagination go wild!

Chapter 4

Creating Your Own Space

Now let's talk about creating your own space... You want to personalize your space and make it a place that you feel comfortable in and one that will make your guests feel welcome.

First, you need some sort of table to do your readings on. The size of your table is up to you. A small round table works best like a 24" - 30" round wooden table with screw-on legs. You can get them in any home improvement center or in most department stores. The detachable legs make it portable. When not in use, it can be disassembled and put in a closet or under your bed to conserve space. A wooden table is the best suggestion for laying out the cards. The natural vibrations of the wood will increase your awareness and help you tune into higher energies. If wood is not available, any table will do. A 24" table is just the right size to hold a full spread, 2 small votive candles and your favorite crystals or incense.

It's not the end of the world if you do not have a table. You can use your nightstand or a snack table, basically anything that is available to you. Garage sales are great for finding an odd table for a few dollars. You may also find some inexpensive candleholders or incense holders at a yard sale as well. One man's trash is another man's treasure!

When laying out your cards it is a good idea to cover your table with a cloth. A silk scarf works well because the cards slide easily on it when they are fanned out. Silk also gives off protective energy. An underskirt, on the table beneath the scarf, looks pleasing to the eye, but this is purely optional and depends on what you like. It covers the bare legs gives the table an elegant look. You can also use the scarf that your cards are wrapped in when they are not in use, as a tablecloth. A black, purple or royal blue silk fabric is intended to enhance the energy of the Tarot Cards and makes the reading more accurate, but any dark color will do.

It is a good idea to add crystals to your table because the stones have energies that promote calmness, grounding, love, etc... based on the type of stone used. Each stone has its own useful properties. Choose your stones wisely. A candle or two also helps to set the mood. Your space should be pleasing to you, help you feel comfortable and at ease, and should allow you to relax. Incense is a good tool for relaxation, too. But, before you use incense it is smart to find out if the person you are reading for has allergies to smoke. Otherwise, they may be coughing through the whole reading.

Remember you want to make your guests feel comfortable too.

Helpful Charts

Here are some charts to aid you in choosing your colors, crystals, and incense for your space.

Color Chart (shows color & purpose)

Violet, Purple - Spiritual, Higher Mind
Indigo – Psychic, Intuition
Blue - Health, Communication, Calm
Green - Money, Earthy, Healing
Pink - Heartfelt Emotion, Healing, Love
Yellow - Intelligence, Source of Power (Sun)
Orange - Soothes Animal Nature
Red - Passion, Expression, Desire, Vitality
White - Innocence, Purity, Cleansing, Angels
Black - Protection, Grounding
Gray - Neutral

Stones & Crystals (shows stone & properties)

Agate - Awakens your inborn talents; balances your body and emotions
Amber - Brings romance, wisdom, calmness
Amethyst - Aids in intuition; peaceful energy
Aventurine - Prosperity; career success; creativity; releases fears and anxieties; tranquility.
Citrine - Helps in problem solving; openness; cheerfulness and joy; healing
Fluorite - Heals many disorders; increases psychic ability; stabilizes disorder

Hematite - Revitalizes and energizes the mind and body
Jade - Wisdom; tranquility; serenity
Malachite - Removes obstructions; clarifies insight; loyalties; peace; protection
Obsidian - Gets rid of negativity; gives inner vision
Quartz Crystal - Brings good energy; aids in clear thinking; amplifies your thoughts
Rose Quartz - Attracts love; promotes compassion; heals the heart; forgiveness
Tiger Eye - A grounding stone; attracts wealth; awareness

Incense Chart (shows purpose & herbs/incense)

Courage - Frankincense or Geranium
Divination - Clove or Hibiscus
Happiness - Lavender or Hyacinth
Health & Healing - Cedarwood, Peppermint, or Rosemary
Love - Lavender, Jasmine, or Cinnamon
Luck - Heather or Pine
Money - Bergamot or Patchouli
Peace - Gardenia, Lilac, or Magnolia
Power - Tangerine, Carnation, or Vanilla
Protection - Frankincense and Myrrh, or Juniper
Psychic Awareness - Clove, Mugwort, or Lemongrass
Purification - Eucalyptus, Musk, or Sandalwood

"Choose your stones wisely."

So You Wanna Read Tarot?

 **Try This:**

These Are A Few Of My Favorite Things

1) What gemstone makes you feel comfortable, powerful or protected? Choose the stone for the qualities you desire.
   My favorite stone is: _____.

2) Is there something that you like to use for support, good luck, or guidance? Like a cross, rabbit's foot, or ring?
   My most treasured item is: _____.

3) Is there a color that you are drawn to or that makes you feel comfortable, strong or powerful? Do you have a favorite?
   My favorite color is: _____.

4) Is there a scent or incense that makes you feel at ease, powerful or protected?
   My favorite incense is: _____.

Now take these four things and incorporate them into your setting or special place for your readings.

D. L. Cocchio

Chapter 5

Where Did It All Start?

To some people, history can be somewhat boring. But I feel it is important to know a little about the history of the tarot so you can appreciate its journey. So I'll keep it brief. If history bores you, skip to Chapter 6, but I think you may find it fascinating.

Many people are curious about the origin of the Tarot cards because the exact date of the discovery of the Tarot Cards is unknown. It is believed that the cards first appeared in Europe during the Renaissance Period. The deck began with just the Major Arcana (those with Roman Numerals on them) and the Minor Arcana (the remaining cards) were added at a later date. The cards themselves are a picture story of the different stages of a soul's journey as it travels through life, from birth to death and to rebirth again.

One theory of origin is that the deck of tarot was secretly used to teach spirituality and religion to people. The word "Arcana" in the title of the "Major

Arcana" means secrets. Early Christians hid this knowledge to make it easier for those in power to teach their own ideas. These "sacred truths" were forbidden to most people and were handed down through secret societies.

"The cards are a picture story of a soul's journey from birth to death."

Here is the most popular folklore about Tarot... Pretending that it was a game, the gypsies in the traveling circus would travel from town to town with their cards. A few of the townspeople would invite the performers into their home after closing time to spend the night with the family. The host family would receive the valuable spiritual and religious teachings of the cards in exchange for a meal and a place to sleep for the tarot readers. There is no historical proof of this, but writers popularized this folktale in 1857.

Another legend says that the deck came with the gypsies when they journeyed to Israel and Greece. When the library in Alexandria was burned, the skilled people of Alexandria were forced to move to Morocco. There were many languages spoken there, making things very confusing. So, the people found it easier to communicate using universal symbols. Supposedly, that is when the symbolic tarot cards were created. These cards represented the universal steps that we all go through to reach spiritual enlightenment. It was a common thread for the people.

So You Wanna Read Tarot?

As far as historical *proof* goes, the first known deck can be traced back to Italy in 1440. The decks called the "Visconti Trumps" were supposedly the predecessors of the tarot decks available today. An artist named Bembo made these decks for the Visconzi-Sforza family in Milan. Tarot cards are an early form of today's playing cards. The cards were named TAROCCO or TAROCCHI. Originally, these cards began as a game for the nobility.

In 1770, Jean-Baptiste Alliette, a diviner and occultist, was the first person to publish the meanings for the cards. He was known as "Etteilla", which was his name spelled backwards. There is not much written history about Etteilla.

In 1781, Antoine Court de Gebelin had a theory that the Trump cards held mystical knowledge in their symbols and were believed to be Egyptian in origin. De Gebelin was part of a secret society of occultists. He believed that the cards were magical symbols of the Egyptian God, Thoth. When the Rosetta stone was discovered it allowed us to translate Egyptian hieroglyphs, however, none of the translations said anything about the tarot cards and did not support the idea that they were Egyptian in origin.

The Tarot was also thought to originate in Israel when Eliphas Levi, who was studying for the priesthood, found ties between the Tarot and the Kabbalah in the 19th century. The Kaballah was a system of mysticism developed by the Hebrews. The Tarot was also tied in with the Tree of Life. It was considered as a key to life itself. When Levi created his own tarot deck, he incorporated religion, the elements, astrology and universal symbols into the cards. In addition, he referenced the bible to aid his students in spiritual enlightenment.

In the 19th century, The Golden Dawn was started in England as a secret occultist society. There were three noteworthy people who were part of the Golden Dawn – S. Liddel Mathers (who later changed his name to MacGregor), Aleister Crowley, and Arthur Waite. Mathers (MacGregor) wrote instructions on the Tarot, combining the ritual material and philosophy that is used for tarot reading today. Aleister Crowley made his own tarot deck called "The Book of Thoth". It had intense symbolism and was very complicated. Crowley also had a bad reputation for dealing with the dark arts. This could be one reason that some people fear the tarot cards are cards from the Devil.

Arthur Waite, on the other hand, had commissioned an American artist, Pamela Colman Smith, to design his tarot deck. He realized that these cards could be used to predict the future. It had a storytelling theme, using the symbols in each scene to tell the story. Waite revived the interest in the Tarot in the 20th century. His deck became the most popular deck of the century because of its easy-to-understand symbolism. It also had colorful characters with familiar stories from myths, fairytales and the bible. For many years the Waite-Smith deck was the only one readily available in the U.S. It was introduced into the Western World in the early 1900"s and became extremely popular during World War I.

In the 1920"s Paul Foster Case from the Golden Dawn founded his own group, "The Builders of the Adytum" or B.O.T.A and created his own deck as well. So, you see, there is proof of Tarot's existence only back to 1440, however there is no physical proof of its origin beyond that. Many people rely on their customs and folktales to tell the origin of the Tarot.

One of the reasons that the church was against the tarot cards was that they didn't want anyone but themselves teaching spirituality and religion. Remember, the Renaissance was a turbulent time when Christianity was spreading rapidly. The church wanted complete control of any teachings of religion.

It has been said that one major misconception is that the Tarot Cards are "the work of the Devil". The cards have been said to be evil, come from "the dark side" and are linked with the occult practices. In fact, all playing cards at the time were known as "cards of the devil" and it had nothing to do with fortune telling. The church had condemned playing cards because the cards were used for gambling, which was considered a sin. Because the tarot deck contained Death and the Devil cards, the churches banned them. To steer people away from other teachings of their religion, the church spread this misconception of the cards being the work of the Devil.

This manufactured rumor is the farthest thing from the truth. It is just human nature to fear the unknown or the unexplained, but tarot cards were not meant to be feared or evil. In fact, they are most spiritual cards and when you are through learning the cards, you will find out for yourself.

"This rumor is the farthest thing from the truth."

 **Try This:**

Make a Personal Tarot Journal

You will probably find it handy to keep a journal as you learn the tarot cards. This way you can refer to it often, remembering those little tidbits that you didn't want to forget. For this, you can either purchase a journal or you can make one of your own and personalize it. You can use one of your extra school notebooks or even an old one that had only a few pages used. Either way, you can personalize the cover with pictures or fabrics, trinkets or stickers, or anything that makes it yours. You will be more likely to write your notes in the book if it is special to you.

Chapter 6

Look A Bit Closer

After choosing a tarot deck, take a look at your cards. The best way to get to know the tarot is by looking at the cards every chance that you get. The more you become familiar with the scenes on the cards, the better off you'll be. They say that every picture is worth a thousand words, which is very true of the tarot. The pictures seem to tell the whole story.

The tarot deck has 78 cards in all. Most decks have similar symbols and meanings. Once you learn the Rider-Waite Tarot Deck, chances are that you will be able to read most tarot decks that you come across. Tarot cards are a useful tool in predicting events or receiving guidance in our daily lives. They are very useful in fortune telling, predictions, and in self-discovery.

"Every picture is worth 1,000 words."

Let's start with the **Major Arcana** cards. These are the ones with the Roman Numerals on them, along with a title, as listed below. The remaining cards are called the **Minor Arcana**. Begin by separating the Major Arcana cards from your deck so that we can concentrate on them. These Major Arcana cards are the most powerful cards in the deck and represent the *major* events in our lives, rather than the everyday events. They outweigh all of the other cards. The word "arcana" actually means secrets.

So You Wanna Read Tarot?

Major Life Events

The 22 Major Arcana are as follows:

0 – The Fool
I – The Magician
II – The High Priestess
III – The Empress
IV – The Emperor
V – The Hierophant
VI – The Lovers
VII – The Chariot
VIII – Strength
IX – The Hermit
X – The Wheel of Fortune
XI – Justice
XII – The Hanged Man
XIII – Death
XIV – Temperance
XV – The Devil
XVI – The Tower
XVII – The Star
XVIII – The Moon
XIX – The Sun
XX – Judgment
XXI – The World

"Every soul goes through each of these stages in its lifetime."

 **Try This:**

Major Arcana Activity

Spread your deck out, face up, on the table in front of you. Group together the **Major Arcana** cards and set the remaining cards aside. It makes it easier if you can put these cards in numerical order starting with 0 – The Fool. Take each of these cards, one by one, say aloud the number and the title, look at the picture for a moment, decide what you think is going on in the scene, then move on to the next one. This is just to get a brief glimpse of what's in your deck. We will look at these closer, later in the book.

It's so important to familiarize yourself with your cards. The more you look at them and touch them, the more you will absorb their meanings. Be sure to make time to try these valuable activities that will help you in your quest to read the Tarot.

 Try This:

Minor Arcana Activity

Now take a look at the other pile of remaining cards. The **Minor Arcana** has 56 cards in all. They represent the everyday events in our lives. There are four suits. You can sort these cards into four piles of cups, wands, pentacles, and swords. These are similar to the suits in a deck of today's playing cards – hearts, clubs, diamonds, and spades. They are broken down further into numbered cards from 1 (being the Ace) to 10 and accompanying court cards, which are Kings, Queens, Knights, and Pages. If you lay the suits next to each other you can compare them with each other in the various suits. For example: put the Kings on the top of each of the piles. Compare the King of Cups, the King of Wands, the King of Pentacles, and the King of Swords to each other. How are they different? How are they similar? Make notes in a notebook. Spread them out on the whole table if you need to. This is a worthwhile activity. Again, we will get to know them a little bit better in the upcoming chapters.

D. L. Cocchio

Chapter 7

The Majors

In this section the Major Arcana cards are shown individually, including a short description of each card, the symbols on the card and what they mean, the true meaning of the card, and what advice to give in a reading for that particular card. Feel free to jot down any additional impressions that you receive from each card in your journal.

Remember, the Major Arcana cards represent the **major** events in a person's life. They draw attention to those events and aid us by giving details to help make that event to run smoothly. Sometimes, being forewarned can make things happen more easily. Since each card can have dozens of meanings, pay attention to what symbol your eyes focus on first when you see that card, as it is usually the most important thing in reading that card. This is what you talk about. Focus on those first symbols.

"Pay attention to what your eyes focus on first."

- ➢ The sample deck I am using is the Rider Tarot deck. I actually prefer the Universal Waite Deck , which is the Rider – Waite cards painted in pastel colors. They are a bit warmer and more inviting in my opinion. They resonate much better with me. Choose the deck that talks to you.

0 – THE FOOL

The Fool is the beginning of the spiritual journey -

beginnings and innocence.

What You See: The card shows a young guy who is not watching where he is going. He seems to be stepping towards the edge of the cliff. His dog is warning him of the danger ahead, but The Fool doesn't seem to care. The Fool is carefree and unafraid. He carries his possessions in a sack tied on a stick over his shoulder, heading towards adventure. The mountains are looming in the background.

The Symbols: Their Meanings:

The Symbols	Their Meanings
White sun	the spiritual sun
White inner robe	the soul, purity, free from desires
Outer robe	the personality, the wheel design on the robe is the wheel of fortune, representing the charkas
His belt	has 12 pearls representing the zodiac, with 7 stars representing time. Time is a restriction put on the Fool.
Yellow boots	yellow is the mind, the air, thus his feet are not yet grounded
Wand (his stick)	a symbol of will
Eagle (on his bag)	represents Scorpio, universal knowledge, death, and rebirth
Wreath	represents the vegetable kingdom
Feather	represents the animal kingdom
Mountains	Snowy mountains - goals to achieve, represents intellect
White Dog	innocence
Colors	yellow – mind (air), blue – psychic, white - purity
Astrology	Uranus – change, awakening

So You Wanna Read Tarot?

The Meaning of the Card:

This card represents you on the first stage of your journey. You are ready to make serious changes, discover faith, and follow your dreams. You are at the crossroads, have an imaginative mind, have a need for caution, are adventurous, and are starting your spiritual journey. You are forced to learn from foolhardiness and being naive. This is the beginning of our journey before life teaches us restrictions. You are a happy-go-lucky, carefree soul. This could be a good thing.

Advice In a Reading: When the Fool shows up in a reading, you will gain a new outlook on life. It is also the beginning of a new cycle in life, a fresh start, a new journey. You should pay more attention to details because you could tend to be careless. The Fool can also depict someone with a carefree attitude and a good sense of adventure, someone not afraid to take a risk. It's time for a change! Tell the person to experience the moment spontaneously!

My Notes:
_____
_____
_____

I – THE MAGICIAN

The Magician is the second stage of the spiritual journey –

will, focus and desire.

What You See: The card shows a young man in a magician's robe standing before a table with his right hand clutching a wand which he points towards the heavens with. His left hand points towards the earth. He is taking power from above and directing it into making things happen below. The four suits of the Minor Arcana are on the table – wands, cups, swords and pentacles, symbolizing the natural elements of fire, water, air and earth. He has everything in front of him to make things happen, he just has to *want* to.

The Symbols: Their Meanings:

The Symbols	Their Meanings
Red Outer Robe	desire
White inner robe	the soul, purity, free from desires
Lemniscate (figure 8)	eternity, has harmony and is conscious of the life cycle
Left hand down, right hand up	makes things happen using both the higher knowledge (from above) and practical earthy knowledge, takes the energy from above & channels it wherever he focuses his attention.
Wand	is a pointer that gives the problem his full attention (double edged – ability to direct the natural forces wherever wanted)
Cup	he collects experience and imagination through observation
Sword	take action - do something or our experience is useless
Pentacle	result, the finished product
Red Rose	earthy desires using the five senses
Serpent's belt	eternity
Astrology	Mercury: communication, mind, speaking, and Math

D. L. Cocchio

The Meaning of the Card:

The Magician card represents man's will in touch with the source above, achieving the knowledge and the power to bring our desires into reality through awareness. He represents our will, focus and desire.

Advice In a Reading: When the Magician shows up in a reading, advise the person that they are going in the right direction and will have the ability to see it through. They have everything in their power to make things happen, and just have to *want* to make it happen. They are talented and should allow themselves to use their talent and power. They also can be an entrepreneur, who with will, focus and faith can succeed. This card is about energy. There is something that needs to be accomplished. Advise the client to apply themselves and focus their energy.

My Notes:
_____
_____
_____
_____
_____

So You Wanna Read Tarot?

II – THE HIGH PRIESTESS

The High Priestess is the third stage of the spiritual journey –

understanding and commitment.

What You See: The card shows the High Priestess sitting on her throne with the Tora, a Hebrew holy book, on her lap. It is only partially unrolled and her cape also covers half of the scroll. She is hiding things from the human eye. There is a crescent moon at her feet and her crown has the three phases of the moon on it – waxing, full, and waning. She sits between two pillars – the black pillar, Boaz, showing negativity in life, and the white pillar, Jakin, showing the positivity in life. There are palms and pomegranates behind her.

The Symbols: Their Meanings:

The Symbols:	Their Meanings:
Color Blue	psychic & intuitive, subconscious
Yellow	intelligence
Pillars	They are from the Temple of Solomon and the tree of life.
Blue Robe	It turns into the river of subconscious that runs through the rest of the cards when femininity is not present.
Full moon crown	crown with waxing and waning moon, shows the ebb & tide, also reincarnation
Cup-shaped moon	receptivity
The palms (behind her)	represents the male
Pomegranates (The fertility fruit)	seeds for the female subconscious to be productive
Cross on her chest	shows balance: equal-armed cross
Lips are sealed	secretive, speaks in symbols
The Tora	divine law, esoteric wisdom; is the link between the seen and unseen. Subconscious remembers it all.
Astrology	The Moon: intuition, feelings, regeneration, reincarnation, dreams a symbol of reflection & duplication.

The Meaning of the Card:

The High Priestess is a virgin who veils the truth and can't see the whole thing. She is committed, intuitive, and represents enlightenment through understanding and memory. The subconscious knows the meanings of the universal symbols - you just need to look at the pictures.

Advice in a Reading: When the High Priestess shows up in a reading, advise the person that there is activity beneath the surface, things are hidden. There are commitment issues. They should use spiritual inspiration, have knowledge and wisdom, and need to pay attention. Say: listen to your psychic intuition. You are a good secret keeper. Go with your gut feeling.

My Notes:

_____

_____

_____

_____

_____

III – THE EMPRESS

The Empress is the fourth stage of the spiritual journey – creative imagination and growth.

What You See: The card shows the Empress sitting on a royal throne, wearing a crown made of 12 stars, and holding a scepter with a globe on top (a woman in charge). We see a field of wheat that is ripening in front of her and a waterfall behind her. She is in the Garden of Eden. The Empress represents growth and fertility, fruitfulness and abundance. She also represents comfort, luxury and is a nurturing mother figure. The Empress is waiting to harvest what she has planted before.

The Symbols:	Their Meanings:
Empress	Mother Earth, Isis, Venus, growth, Reproduction, Mother Nature
Heart symbol (on shield)	represents Goddess of Love (Venus)
Garden	nature, growth, fertility
Wheat field	represents fertility and is sacred to Isis
Stream	represents the unconscious mind
Myrtle wreath	sacred to Venus
7 pearls	7 chakras, 7 planets
12 stars (on crown)	12 signs of zodiac, dominion of the Zodiac, dominion of the world
scepter	represents power and authority
Lips are sealed	secretive, speaks in symbols
Astrology	Venus : symbolizes harmony and love

The Meaning of the Card:

The Empress is productive activities and creative imagination in the subconscious. She stands for fertility, fruitfulness and abundance. She joins desire (The Magician) and understanding (The High Priestess) with creative imagination (Empress) so that you can visualize creating these things in your life with feminine energy. The future is yours to create. A woman is in charge and her power is visualization. She stands for maternal urges, mother, grounding, artist, woman, creative thought, feminine energy, abundance, love, and nurturing. Often the card can represent a person's mother or wife. This person values home and family and appreciates fine things. It can also indicate a pregnancy. Again – talk about what your eyes focus on.

Advice in a Reading: When the Empress shows up in a reading advise the person to go for it! Something from the past finally pays off. Creativity is involved. A bright idea may have occurred to you. Keep up the good work! If reading for a woman, this card can represent her own fertility and femininity, growth and abundance. The cards around it will tell you what area the growth will take place (pentacles – money, cups – love and friendship, swords – mental perception, rods or wands – creativity). It is a fertile time for affairs of the heart.

My Notes:
_____
_____
_____
_____
_____

IV – THE EMPEROR

The Emperor is the fifth stage of the spiritual journey –

reason, vision, stability and authority.

What You See: The card shows the Emperor or the 'Man in Charge' sitting on a throne that is decorated with rams' heads on the arms and back of the chair (emblems of Mars). In his right hand he holds a scepter of an Egyptian Ankh (the cross of life). In his left hand he holds a globe (a symbol of the world). On his shoulder is another Ram's Head. He sits with an air of authority. We see bare mountains looming in the background.

So You Wanna Read Tarot?

The Symbols: Their Meanings:

Ram's head	a symbol of Aries, Mars
Ankh	Venus' symbol – everlasting life
Globe	Shows that with the feminine power of love he can balance spirit & matter, giving true ruling power
The River of Subconscious	This river runs through the card.
White beard	represents a wise man who manifests things
Mountains	achieves aspirations
Globe & cross	rulership and control of the material world, authority, law
Blue lining of robe	psychic sense
Blue armor	trusts his intuition
Red outer robe	desire
Orange color	earthy desires (on the mountains -it means achieving them)
Yellow crown	intelligence
Astrology	Aries: symbolizes adventure, impulsiveness, headstrong and active.

The Meaning of the Card: This is a card about the powers that be. The Emperor demonstrates kingship, leadership, government, control, power, intelligence, reason vision, manifestation, the boss, and going places. The Emperor symbolizes authority figures – fathers, bosses, executives, leaders, and politicians.

Advice In a Reading: Tell them "You need order in your life". When this card shows up, it usually means that an issue of authority will come up in which the person must confront his attitudes toward outside power. If he has been a rebel in the past, he may overreact to the need for rules. If he has been over-intimidated by authority, he may experience anxiety about pleasing authority figures. He must follow the rules and play the game in order to receive acknowledgement from the person in charge. It can also indicate a man of authority.

My Notes:

_____

_____
_____

_____

_____

V – THE HIEROPHANT

The Hierophant is the sixth stage of the spiritual journey – using traditional, established values.

What You See: The card shows the Hierophant, a religious man on a throne wearing the triple crown of a pope and holding a scepter of a triple cross. He is seated between 2 pillars. At his feet are crossed keys, a gold one for solar energy and a silver one for unseen forces of the moon. Two priests kneel before him, one in a garment with white lilies and the other with red roses. He is the ruling power of external religion (the masses).

The Symbols: Their Meanings:

The Symbols	Their Meanings
Triple crown	spirit, soul, & body, the creative, formative, and material worlds
Pillars	mercy and severity
Keys	Gold- the sun; silver – the moon; It unlocks the gate of the inner temple of intuition.
Priest in white lily garment	represents thought & knowledge
Priest in red roses garment	represents desire
Inner robe – white	purity and the blue part- psychicness
Outer robe – red	desire
Yellow crown	knowledge, intelligence
Astrology	Taurus – symbolizes earthiness, practicality, stubborness, and determination

So You Wanna Read Tarot?

The Meaning of the Card: This card stands for traditional, established values, sometimes indicating marriage. The card means stability, being dependable, conservative, and being a teacher. It teaches us that we have inner hearing, which is our inner teacher (intuition). The Hierophant may also represent a religious ceremony. It can indicate conventional religious activities. It stands for the need to be told by an external authority what is morally right and wrong.

Advice In a Reading: Tell them to have faith! Believe! Although all the things around you are not always in your control, do the best you can with what you've got and let the rest take care of itself. Do things "the traditional way." Someone is looking out for you! You're looking for advice from a traditional source. Listen to the advice.

My Notes:
_____
_____
_____
_____

VI THE LOVERS

The Lovers is the seventh stage of the spiritual journey –

choices with confidence and harmony.

What You See: In this card the sun is shining down upon a man and a woman, Adam and Eve. They are being watched over by the Angel Raphael who has influence on them. The Tree of Life is behind the man, bearing 12 fruits and the Tree of Knowledge of Good and Evil stands behind the woman. We see that the man looks towards the woman and the woman looks towards the angel. The man does not make direct contact with the angel (super-consciousness), but rather goes through Eve (the subconscious). This is the card of human love.

The Symbols: Their Meanings:

The Symbols:	Their Meanings:
Archangel Raphael	a healing angel that represents spirit and the super-consciousness
Clouds	We are separated (or clouded) from the superconscious.
Man	represents the conscious side, the male life force
Woman	represents the subconscious, the female life force
Tree of life	man has 12 horoscope flowers on the tree of life, 12 months
Nudity	They have nothing to hide from each other.
Mountains closer	Goals are getting closer.
Astrology	Gemini – symbolizing communications, changes – both scattered and superficial.

D. L. Cocchio

The Meaning of the Card: This card sometimes can signify true love, depending on the surrounding cards. It shows the need to discriminate between two choices using both consciousness and intuition. It represents beauty and inner harmony, making choices, merging of opposites, romance or a romantic encounter.

Advice In a Reading: Be ready for love, if there are cup cards near it in the spread. Sometimes this card tells of romance coming and meeting that special someone to complement you. It will open doors for you. You must make an important decision between two choices because a choice is being offered, but you need to know what you really want for you to choose correctly.

My Notes:

_____

_____

_____

_____

_____

_____

VII THE CHARIOT

The Chariot is the eighth stage of the spiritual journey – controlling senses, being in charge.

What You See: The card shows a prince riding in a chariot pulled by two Sphinxes, holding the "wand of authority and will" in his right hand. The shield on the front of the chariot has the symbol of the union of positive and negative forces. The white sphinx stands for mercy and the black sphinx stands for justice (our senses). He wears astrological signs on his belt and there are moons on his shoulder armor. We see two homes in the background.

The Symbols: Their Meanings:

Symbol	Meaning
Chariot	our vehicle – our body
Wings	inner self – the soul
Sphinxes	our senses
Belt	signs of the astrology symbols
Moons on shoulders	very much affected by the tides, death and rebirth.
Stars on canopy	cosmic energy, power of life
Star crown	symbol of one in charge
Wand	authority & will (from the Magician)
Two homes in background	He is the protector of the home.
Astrology	Cancer – symbolizing nurturing, intuitiveness, and dependence

The Meaning of the Card: This card stands for taking the reigns and being in charge. The prince controls his chariot without reigns. It stands for conquest, achieving greatness, being initiative and determined. This card represents triumph and success. It can also mean an important trip, travel, or someone is coming to visit. Sometimes it can mean a new car (if you focus on the chariot). This card can also represent the protector, a family person. We must control our senses with our mind.

Advice In a Reading: Full speed ahead! Focus your energy and concentration on your goal. You are responsible for your life, nobody else is. Go get 'em. You have the energy and drive to accomplish your goal. Take control of the situation. Sometimes a trip by land is indicated.

My Notes:
_____
_____
_____
_____
_____

VIII Strength

Strength is the ninth stage of the spiritual journey –

courage and conviction.

What You See: The card shows a woman with the eternal life symbol above her head, closing the mouth of the lion. She has comforted the beast. She holds inner steadiness and can calm the savage beast. There is a chain of roses around her waist. She appears to have harmony over opposing forces between spiritual and animal natures (our higher and lower self). We see mountains in the distance.

The Symbols: Their Meanings:

Lemniscates	an eternal life symbol that shows she is in control, thanks to the spirit above
White robe	represents purity
Chain of roses	It is a union of desire and desire is in union with the spiritual side.
Red roses	desire
White robe	purity
Blue mountains	psychic energy
Woman	represents the subconscious having spiritual control over the lion – representing the balance of forces.
The lion	represents passions and animal nature of man, we need our animal instincts to survive.
Yellow sky	represents intelligence
Astrology	Leo- symbolizing attention-getting, courageousness, & insensitiveness.

D. L. Cocchio

The Meaning of the Card: This card stands for allowing your higher self to dictate your desires. Know that you don't need to question your motives. It shows that you are balanced and have control over your animal instincts. Be calm. This card is all about soothing the savage beast.

Advice In a Reading: When this card turns up in your reading, it suggests that you are feeling in good health and have inner confidence. It is also advised that when dealing with others, kindness, compassion and firmness will help out now. *You can bring harmony out of conflict.* Strength and patience will help in matters. Show what you are capable of and let your enjoyment of life conquer adversity.

My Notes:
_____
_____
_____
_____
_____

So You Wanna Read Tarot?

IX The Hermit

The Hermit is the tenth stage of the spiritual journey –

self-discovery through inner reflection.

What You See: The card shows the Hermit carrying a lantern, searching for something. He wears a long, gray monk's robe and is also lighting the way for the people below him because he is on a snow-topped mountain peak. In his lantern is a 6-pointed star. The man has a long, white beard and looks very wise. His eyes seem closed, almost as if meditating. His wand provides stability.

The Symbols: Their Meanings:

The Symbols	Their Meanings
Lamp	the lamp of truth or the light
6-pointed star	The Seal of Solomon, the ray of cosmic energy, or the way to enlightenment
Wand	will
Gray robe	neutralization
White hair	wise man or woman
Blue sky	subconscious presence that the hermit can delve into
Mountain top	has reached a spiritual peak
Astrology	Virgo – symbolizing the analytical, orderly, and logical

The Meaning of the Card: The Hermit looks at where he has come from (introspection) and is ready to shed light to anyone trying to find the way (through meditation). He holds the lamp of wisdom to guide others to greater awareness. The hermit represents a period of contemplation and meditation. The Hermit is a teacher that encourages discipline, study and schooling. The Hermit refers to self-discovery through inner reflection. Although there are many paths up the mountain, they all lead to the same place.

Advice In a Reading: It is time to do some introspection, to look "within" and try to find out who you really are and where you are going. Take some time for yourself and do some soul-searching. Are you on the right path? If not, then make the appropriate changes. It might be a good time to take classes or look to a teacher for direction. Meditate and listen to your inner self.

My Notes:
_____
_____
_____

X WHEEL OF FORTUNE

The Wheel of Fortune is the eleventh stage of the spiritual journey – *change happening, already put in motion.*

What You See: The card shows a wheel rotating in the center of this card – the wheel of change. Just like a carnival wheel, you take your chances. Taking a chance always encourages change. This represents cause and effect, so by putting the wheel in motion it causes things to happen. A snake, a jackal and a sphinx are riding the wheel. At the four corners of the card are the four mythical creatures of the bible. The bull also represents Taurus, the lion is Leo, the eagle is Scorpio, and the Angel is Aquarius - all fixed signs of the zodiac.

The Symbols: Their Meanings:

The Symbols	Their Meanings
8-spoked wheel	represents the motion of the universe and life within it
Books (in the 4 corners)	knowledge learned which puts the wheel in motion
Wings	knowledge that has set them free
Signs on the wheel	symbols of alchemy = Mercury (on top), Sulfur (right), Salt (left), and Water - Aquarius – dissolution (at bottom).
T-A-R-O-T	letters around the wheel that spell tarot infinitely
Sphinx w/ sword	He is taking action with his sword and putting things in motion.
3 circles (the wheel)	body, soul, spirit
Snake	consciousness
Jackal	Egyptian God Hermes
Astrology	Planet Jupiter – symbolizing optimum and abundance

D. L. Cocchio

The Meaning of the Card: The huge wheel in the center showing us impending change as it is in motion. The books in the hands of the creatures in the four corners of the card signify knowledge learned which puts the wheel in motion. The wings on the creatures mean that this knowledge has been set free. As the wheel rotates, it changes lower forms of consciousness (represented by the snake) to the Egyptian God Hermes (Jackal-headed form), who represents man behind his personality, wisdom, with the power to change life. This almost always tells of change happening for the better. The universe responds to your desires, once you set things in motion. We are always moving, we come down from a higher source and spend the rest of our time here trying to get back.

Advice In a Reading: A job is in store for you – take a gamble, luck is with you. Take a risk and it will put things in motion for you. You need to change your life to make use of creative energy. A new cycle of life is about to push you in a different direction. Learn how to flow with the ups and downs of life. Sudden unexpected changes are happening. Good fortune, success, or a turn of luck.

So You Wanna Read Tarot?

My Notes:

_____
_____
_____
_____
_____
_____
_____

XI JUSTICE

Justice is the twelfth stage of the spiritual journey –
balance and effect.

What You See: The card shows the Justice (a judge) seated in front of two pillars from which a veil is draped between. It is shielding what is behind the judge, the pillars of justice open into an area that symbolizes the higher inner mind, where all knowledge resides. In her left hand are the scales of justice, in her right hand is a double-edged sword that is able to cut both ways. Swords indicate that action needs to be taken. She wears a red robe with a green cape and a crown upon her head. She looks determined that justice

So You Wanna Read Tarot?

will be done.

The Symbols: Their Meanings:

The Symbols	Their Meanings
Scales	The scales of justice represent balanced judgment, and equilibrium.
Circle within a square (cape)	This holds her cape on and signifies spirit (intuition).
Cube (she sits on)	signifies matter (reason), she uses intuition and reason to judge
Two pillars	positive and negative energy
Sword	in defense of justice, a double-edge sword can create and also destroy
Blue on sword	knowledge of superconscious, cuts away what you don't need
Purple drape in back	represents inner mind
Yellow color	represents intellect and the subconscious
Red outer robe	desire for balance and harmony to happen
Astrology	Libra – symbolizing balance and conventional things

The Meaning of the Card: Justice will be done, good or bad. The sword of knowledge cuts away what we no longer need by using what the Hermit decided that we want in our life. By cutting things out we leave room for more good things to come into our life, making us balanced. Justice is the effect part of "cause and effect". Whatever you put into motion with the Wheel of Fortune will be judged and experienced here.

Advice In a Reading: Balance is required and justice will be done. The right decision must be made in order for it to work out. Cut away any unwanted baggage. This can also mean good news in court. Take responsibility for your decisions. What you give will come back to you three times over. This can also represent Karma.

My Notes:
_____
_____
_____
_____
_____
_____

So You Wanna Read Tarot?

XII THE HANGED MAN

The Hanged Man is the thirteenth stage of the spiritual

journey – *pause now, take action later.*

What You See: The card shows the Hanged Man hanging from the gallows by his leg. His arms are folded behind him, while his head and arms form a triangle and his legs form a cross. There is a glow around his head as if in thought. He wears a blue garment with red stockings. The hanged man has achieved some spirituality but still is bound by material things. He can escape but chooses not to and just needs to hang out, for now.

The Symbols: Their Meanings:

Triangle	His arms and head form a triangle with the point down which means he is still bound by materialism.
Red stockings	These represent his earthly desires.
Outer blue garment	This signifies his desire to make changes.
Yellow halo	He is deep in thought, intellect.
Loose twine around leg	The twine is loose around his leg and he can easily get out, but chooses to hang out and think.
Green leaves	Leaves symbolize growth – there is room for growth from this experience.
Hangman's Tree	The man is "hanging out", not making any rash decisions, pausing for a moment.
Astrology	Neptune – symbolizing everything mystical, creative, dependent, and addictive.

The Meaning of the Card: Decisions need to be thought over and suspended temporarily. Surrender to a higher power. You have a need to reverse your life. The Hanged Man is trying to reverse his life. He is going within himself and asking for help. Sometimes this can mean addictions and co-dependency. Plan now and take action later.

Advice In a Reading: Tell them to chill out! Don't make any quick decisions. Now is the time to hang out and think things over. You can create the life you want, if you plan now. *Reverse* your life and allow spirit to guide you into making things happen. Look at yourself through the eyes of others. Be ready for some personal sacrifice.

My Notes:
___
___
___
___
___
___

XIII DEATH

Death is the fourteenth stage of the spiritual journey –

transformation and regeneration.

What You See: Death (the skeleton) is wearing armor and is riding a white horse. He is holding a black flag with a white, 5-petal rose, signifying life force. In the background, the sun is rising between the two towers. The rider is trampling everything in its path. This card represents death of the old self and the old ways. It is not always physical death, although it can mean that, at times. It stands for regenerating the soul.

The Symbols: Their Meanings:

The Symbols:	Their Meanings:
5-petal rose	signifies life force
Rising sun	everlasting life
2 towers in back	represents putting fears behind you to make way for change
Priest with gloves	Christianity is dying out; the Piscean age dying out and coming into the Aquarian age.
Huge blue river	subconscious level, represents the River Styx
Skeleton	transformation and reincarnation
White horse	pure of body and spirit
Astrology	Scorpio : symbolizing compulsiveness, intensity, and secretive

The Meaning of the Card: This card says that a transformation and change is sorely needed. The changes can be physical or mental. New opportunities – out with the old and in with the new. Clean out old closets. Rebirth and renewal is evident. Through death we realize we are more than just our bodies.

Advice In a Reading: Tell them it is time to de-clutter your environment, clean out closets and get rid of the old to make way for the new. Transformation and change is needed. If you are stuck in old patterns, make changes. Change your ways. A part of your life is dying off and changing. And you will be moving in a new direction. Let go of the old in order to get a second chance.

My Notes:
_____
_____
_____
_____
_____
_____

So You Wanna Read Tarot?

XIV Temperance

Temperance is the fifteenth stage of the spiritual journey –

patience and moderation.

What You See: The card shows the angel of the sun - Michael, pouring water from one cup into another, almost as if mixing the fluid. His red feathery wings take up a good portion of the card. Michael has one foot on a rock and the other in the water. Behind him are tall grasses and yellow lilies. On the other side is a path that leads to the mountains, with the sun in the form of a crown at the end.

The Symbols: ## Their Meanings:

The Symbols:	Their Meanings:
Triangle in square (on chest)	This is the sign of the Book of Tarot and also refers to the 7 chakras.
One foot in water, other on earth	It shows that he balances between the conscious and subconscious and he is just as comfortable with the spirit side as he is with the physical side.
Lilies	Lilies are a sign of achievement.
The sun	Shaped like a crown at the end of the path, this means to take the path between wisdom and understanding to achieve the crown in glory.
Water/ Stream	Water also signifies emotions, here the emotions can be kept balanced
Astrology	Sagittarius – symbolizing ethics, outgoing and straight-forwardness.

The Meaning of the Card: This card stands for balancing and moderation, taking things one day at a time. Michael is pouring the liquid of life from the cup of subconscious into the cup of the conscious. This gives you mental balance by choosing the middle path. Michael understands when you screw up.

Advice In a Reading: Tell them to take things in stride with moderation. Take little baby steps in what you are doing. Try to master self-control. Make adjustments and test things out. Be patient, go slow. Cool off a little. Don't be extreme. Take the middle path.

My Notes:
_____
_____
_____
_____
_____
_____

D. L. Cocchio

XV The Devil

The Devil is the sixteenth stage of the spiritual journey –

bad habits, your downfall, material things that bind you.

What You See: The card shows a Devil with wings perched on a half of a cube, with an upside-down pentagram on his head. He has the head and hind quarters of a goat, the ears of a donkey, the torso of a man, and the feet of a bird. His right hand is raised with his fingers parted and carries a torch in his left hand . A man and a woman are loosely chained to the devil's perch with the chains so loose that they could escape very easily, but they don't realize it. Both are wearing horns and are naked. The woman has grapes for a tail (fertility) and the man has fire (desire) for his tail.

The Symbols: Their Meanings:

The Symbols	Their Meanings
Upside-down pentagram	shows that man's place in the universe is reversed
Half of a cube	The devil sits on only half of a cube, meaning that he only sees half of the matter.
Flaming torch	His flaming torch is upside-down and is a symbol of black magic and destruction.
Chains	The chains holding the man and woman captive are loose enough to remove, which means the stuff that binds us is imaginary.
Donkey ears	stubborn and stupid
Goat head	materialism
Bat wings	darkness
Horns on heads	bound to animal nature
Astrology	Planet Saturn – symbolizing restrictiveness, disciplined and materialistic.

The Meaning of the Card: This Devil represents our own character flaws – the things that we tend to do, that we hate ourselves when we do it, but can't help it. Examples are bad habits like gambling, drinking, smoking, spending too much money, eating, drugs, sex, and lying. All of the things that always get us into trouble when we tend to slip into them such as being too nice, or even procrastinating can be a vise, too.

Advice In a Reading: You need to be honest with yourself. Be careful of your bad habits. But, if you face the problem, you can overcome it. You feel trapped. Try to change your patterns. This card may signify vices such as nail biting, squeezing pimples, watching too much television, overeating, temptation, obsession, etc... You know that you shouldn't be doing it, yet you continue to do it all the same. I know, we all have these things, but try not to let it get in the way. Try to keep a lid on it. If you can admit to it, you can change it.

My Notes:
_____
_____

XVI The Tower

The Tower is the seventeenth stage of the spiritual journey –
disruption and change.

What You See: The card shows a tower that is being struck by lightning from out of nowhere. The crown of material thought falls from the tower as the tower is crumbling, making way for a new one. Flames are shooting from the tower and people are bailing out. The picture shows smoke and fire everywhere.

The Symbols: Their Meanings:

The Symbols	Their Meanings
The tower	This is like the Tower of Babel in the Bible. It crumbles down.
Crown	This signifies personal willpower and ego.
Lightning	It represents an awakening, clear vision.
Striking (lightning)	When lightning strikes, nothing can stop it.
Smoke and fire	signs of trouble spreading
Astrology	Mars – symbolizing boldness, anger, and aggression

The Meaning of the Card: This card stands for major, drastic change that is out of your control. It is going to happen no matter what. It's an awakening to our higher purpose. It's the "kick in the butt" card. Somewhere there is a lesson to be learned in it. Just get through it and you will so much better. Remember the Phoenix always rises from the ashes.

Advice In a Reading: You are advised that a major change that is out of your control is coming your way. Try to prepare for it as best as you can and it will tend to make things a little bit easier for you. Accept the changes and rebuild. Continue going forward from there. Plans will not go as expected.

My Notes:
_____
_____
_____
_____
_____
_____

D. L. Cocchio

XVII The Star

The Star is the eighteenth stage of the spiritual journey –

your hopes, dreams, and faith.

What You See: The card shows a woman who is kneeling on the earth with one foot on the water and the other on land. She is pouring the water of life from the two pitchers, one onto the earth (matter) and the other into the pool of water (universal consciousness). The waters seem to connect. A bird sits in the tree in the background with a huge star with 8 points in the sky above her head, surrounded by seven smaller stars. We see purple mountains far in the background.

The Symbols: Their Meanings:

The Symbols:	Their Meanings:
Woman	represents mother nature, youth, and beauty
8-pointed star	symbolizes cosmic energy (the power of life)
7 smaller stars	denotes the 7 chakras or energy centers of the body
5 streams on the land	the five senses
Tree	the mind
Bird	Ibis- Hermes' bird from Greek Mythology, represents thought
Purple mountains	achievements earned
Astrology	Aquarius – symbolizing friendliness, humanistic and innovativeness

The Meaning of the Card: This card tells us that by releasing negativity and blockages it allows us to realize our true star potential. It is beneficial to meditate and connect to the source (the cosmic energy). We must love ourselves and take care of our bodies if we wish to fulfill our life's purpose.

Advice In a Reading: The Star represents hope, taking care of oneself, having courage, reaching for the stars and achieving them. You are on the right path to having your hopes and dreams come true. Feel optimistic and be full of confidence because you will get it!

My Notes:
_____
_____
_____
_____
_____
_____

So You Wanna Read Tarot?

XVIII The Moon

The Moon is the nineteenth stage of the spiritual journey –

Dangers and hidden things that surface.

What You See: The card shows a wolf and a dog howling at the moon. The moon is a very secretive card. A crayfish is creeping out of the water, sneaking up on the two animals. The moon hangs low in the sky and shows all 3 phases of the moon – waxing, waning and full. With its rays, the sun is trying to light the way to the path that runs between the two towers, heading towards the mountains.

The Symbols: Their Meanings:

3 phases of the moon	this symbolizes the body, soul, and spirit
Wolf	He acts on his own instinct.
Dog	He is a wolf that has evolved through contact with man.
Crayfish	A symbol for deception; things may not be what they appear to be.
Towers	egos and fears, we must go through the towers to the path of achievement.
Astrology	Pisces – symbolizing compassion, vulnerability, sensitivity, and creativeness

The Meaning of the Card: This card stands for imagination, intuition, and dreams. It signifies hidden things creeping up unexpectedly, also deception, fears, and illusion. It symbolizes those things that haunt us like secrets, buried memories, compulsions, and our fears.

Advice In a Reading: Listen to your dreams to uncover hidden meanings. Things may creep up on you when you least expect it. Hidden things or secrets are going to surface. Watch out for dishonesty and deception. Beware of people with ulterior motives. Face your fears and you will be guided in the right direction.

My Notes:
_____
_____
_____
_____
_____
_____

XIX The Sun

The Sun is the twentieth stage of the spiritual journey –

extreme happiness and satisfaction.

What You See: The card shows a happy, naked child riding a white horse, and holding a huge red flag. The child is riding bareback, and seems to have perfect balance (of the conscious and subconscious). Four sunflowers are in the background, while the large sun fills the sky. A gray garden wall stands behind him.

The Symbols: Their Meanings:

The Symbols	Their Meanings
4 sunflowers	They symbolize the 4 kingdoms of nature – animal, mineral, vegetable, and human.
Horse	represents life energy
Sun	the source of life
Happy child	unconditional love
Naked child	us, children of God, the way we came into this world
Banner, flag	action and vibration
Walled garden	matter made by man - the child is leaving it
Astrology	Planet- The Sun – symbolizing independence, individuality, and consciousness.

The Meaning of the Card: This card stands for good luck and achievement. It symbolizes regeneration and growth, wisdom, joy, personal growth, success, many blessings, good health, and the fulfillment of goals. It is a happy card.

Advice In a Reading: Whatever you start now, you will succeed in it. The sun is lighting up every path you take. You will have good luck, good health, and have many blessings. It signifies contentment. Your optimism and success could be infectious and could inspire others.

My Notes:

_____

_____

_____

_____

_____

_____

XX Judgement

The Judgement is the twenty-first stage of the spiritual

journey – *an awakening and leap of faith.*

What You See: The card shows an angel from the heavens blowing a trumpet, donning a healing cross on the flag of his trumpet. He is the angel Gabriel. The dead people are rising from their coffins that are floating in the water. They are hearing his call and raising their arms towards the angel with a "Let go, let God" attitude, ready to take a leap of faith.

The Symbols: Their Meanings:

The Symbols	Their Meanings
7 rays from the horn	This represents the 7 chakras.
Coffins	It represents being born again.
Equal armed cross (flag)	a sign of the balance of forces
Man	represents the consciousness
Woman	represents the sub-conscious
Child	A child is a symbol of spirit and matter combined.
Astrology	Planet- Pluto – symbolizing regeneration, metamorphosis, and power

The Meaning of the Card: This card stands for an awakening or a renewal. It means taking a leap of faith or a rite of passage by being born again. It signifies healing, liberation, and letting our higher self guide us or letting God guide us.

Advice In a Reading: Tell them that valuable lessons have been learned. Everything that caused you trouble before will disappear. It's time to realize your path in life and get your reward. A more positive cycle is beginning for you. Have a "Let go - let God" attitude. Know that God has a purpose for you.

My Notes:
_____
_____
_____
_____
_____
_____

XXI The World

The World is the twenty-second and last stage of the spiritual

journey – *success and promises assured.*

What You See: The card shows a dancing woman in the center who carries a wand in each hand. She is encircled by a wreath made of interwoven leaves, tied together by red ribbons. Each of the four corners has a fixed sign of the zodiac and stand for the elements : *Taurus* - represented by the bull (earth), *Leo* - represented by the lion (fire), *Scorpio* -

represented by the angel (water), and A*quarius* - represented by the eagle (air).

The Symbols: Their Meanings:

The Symbols	Their Meanings
Wreath	symbolizes nature is on her course
Red ribbon	tied in a figure eight, means eternal life
Clouds	These appear in the four corners and veils slightly what is in those corners; you only get a glimpse.
Two wands	They stand for evolution and involution, meaning that the woman herself has changed through her own involvement.
Signs of the zodiac	signifies the blending together of the best qualities of these four signs
Astrology	Capricorn – symbolizing domination, seriousness, and hard work

D. L. Cocchio

The Meaning of the Card: This card stands for success, completion and fulfillment. Once you realize your limitations, you can be successful. Rewards have been earned for hard work. An understanding of the issues that concern the person has finally happened. It can signify world travel. You've completed the spiritual journey. *Congratulations!*

Advice In a Reading: You will be very successful once you realize where your limitations are - what you can and cannot do. You will overcome all obstacles moving forward, but using your limitations as strengths. You will be reaching your goal, getting that great job, or being accepted to that college. Enjoy your achievements. You finally did it!

My Notes:

_____

_____

_____

_____

_____

_____

So You Wanna Read Tarot?

Chapter 8

The Suits

Now, let's take a closer look at the four suits of the tarot deck. The suits are Wands, Cups, Swords and Pentacles. These symbols are comparable to the suits in a regular playing card deck or poker deck – clubs, hearts, spades, and diamonds. If you learn the elements and explanations of each suit of the tarot deck, you will already be able to tell a little about the card right off the bat. This little bit of knowledge can be quite helpful.

The Suits

Wands, Cups, Swords & Pentacles

Wands

Represents: Wands usually represent fire, creativity, passions and desires. They are ideas, original thought, and growth.

Lots of them: When there are many wands in a reading it means that things are in the thinking stage or the very first stages of development.

Cups

Represents: Cups usually represent emotions, water, nurturing and intuition. They are the feelings (emotion) between the original idea and the next stage, which is action.

Lots of them: When there are many cups in a reading it means that things are mainly being felt emotionally.

Swords

Represents: Swords usually represent action, air, communications, and struggle. They symbolize the struggle that a person has to go through to turn thought into reality.

Lots of them: When there are many swords in a reading, it shows lots of activity because swords are the last stages of effort before the ending result.

Pentacles

Represents: Pentacles usually represent money, security, the earth and energy. When you think of pentacles, think of making things happen. They are the result.

Lots of them: When there are many pentacles in a reading, it means that things are finally happening or ending. Hooray!

Tips For Telling Timing With The Cards

Timing is usually very hard to feel, but if the person you are reading wants to know when something will happen, think about the matter at hand and pull another card from the pile as your timing card.

- The <u>number</u> on the card tells the **how many** of days, weeks or months. Use your intuition to figure out which of these it is. The number can also represent the number of the month beginning with January = 1.

- The <u>suit</u> of the card has been known to tell **what** measure of time it actually will be – in days, weeks or months.

♦ Note: Many resources switch these around. These are the most common:

Cups = days, Wands = weeks,
Swords = years, Pentacles = months

➢ The <u>scene</u> on the card can also indicate the **season** it will happen in.

Cups = summer, Wands = spring,

Swords = winter, Pentacles = autumn

➢ Let your intuition guide you in determining if it is showing you the answer as a season or in days, weeks, or months and take it from there.

➢ If your timing card is a Major Arcana card, it means it will happen now or quite soon.

Chapter 9

The King And His Court

The King, Queen, Knight and Page are part of the sixteen Court Cards in the deck of Tarot. These cards can represent many things. Pages are essentially the **seeds** of opportunities being planted. Knights **bring forth** this opportunity. Queens and Kings can **represent a man or woman** in your life that are strong in the areas that the suits are explaining. Take a look at the descriptions of the Page, Knight, Queen and King and try to envision these types of people. Sometimes if you associate the card with a person that you know of that "type" it may help you to remember it better.

The King and His Court

16 Court Cards

The Court Cards are the King, Queen, Knight and Page. There are Court Cards in each suit – wands, cups, swords and pentacles.

Pages

Represents: The Pages are the beginnings of opportunities and communication in the area that the suit represents. An example would be that the Page of Cups represents communication opportunities in the area of Love or Emotions. They can also represent young children with the hair and eye coloring seen on the card.

Knights

Represents: The Knights stand for taking action, often of an opportunity presented to you. They can also represent younger men, immature males, or tomboys. The hair and eye coloring on the card can represent someone in your life with those features. Use your intuition to determine which clues to use.

Queens

Represents: The Queens usually represent our feminine side. They are our caregivers, mothers, co-workers, wives and nurturers. They can represent a strong woman in your life or merely stand for a woman around you with similar hair and eye coloring.

Kings

Represents: The Kings show our masculine side. They are bosses, fathers, husbands and authority figures. They are the one in charge. They may even represent a man around you with those eye and hair colorings or features as the card depicts.

Sometimes Court Cards represent the type of person shown on the card. Wands are usually people with red or fair hair, blue eyes and fair skin. Cups are people with light brown hair and blue or hazel eyes. Swords represent people with brown or black hair and dark eyes.

Pentacles are people with white or dark hair and fair or dark skin.

Think of people with those features as the card turns up. Again, use your intuition and let it guide you to the symbols shown on the card. Speak about what your eyes focus on when a particular card turns up. That is what the card is meant to represent. Trust your gut feeling, first instincts are always right. Just go with that meaning. - you will find that you are right. The key here is to learn to trust yourself.

Each Page, Queen and King is also linked to an astrological sign (see next page) . Sometimes the astrological sign connected to the card can shed some light on its meaning. It may symbolize a person corresponding to the astrological sign that you know. Once again, let your intuition guide you. It all comes with practice.

Astrology Tarot Chart

The Court Cards by Suit

(Quick Notes)

Wands

* FIRE * CREATIVITY * PASSION * DESIRES *

Page of Wands - You should seek a new direction for growth and learning. The page brings news or **seeds** of business or creativity.

Knight of Wands - Knights bring **change** – an offer of a job, change in business/home. You are willing to act.

Queen of Wands - Inspiring others with leadership, the Queen is a businesswoman - nurture her passion. She inspires others.

King of Wands - The King is a stubborn, noble, hot-tempered man. He shows signs of passion. Acknowledge the ability you have to manifest your dreams.

So You Wanna Read Tarot?

CUPS
* WATER * EMOTIONS * NURTURING * INTUITION *

Page of Cups - The Page brings news or **seeds** of the beginnings of an emotional nature. (emotions/love) Be open to communications of your emotions (love letters). Be open to new relationships. Be willing to risk loving, romantic invitations.

Knight of Cups - Knights bring **offers**. He is bringing an offer of love, comfort, or proposal. Be willing to act on dreams. He is full of emotion.

Queen of Cups - She nurtures emotions and has tenderness, such as a caregiver. The Queen is a psychic, a woman who nurtures through her creative and intuitive psychic sense.

King of Cups - The King is a family man, but has to balance his emotions. He is giving and loving, a father figure.

SWORDS

* AIR * STRUGGLE* THOUGHTS * COMMUNICATIONS *
*IDEAS * WRITERS * DEFENDERS *

Page of Swords - This Page brings a verbal **seed**, or start of communication. He tells you to begin **action** and communication. He can represent someone who is defensive as well. You need to put things into words.

Knight of Swords - The Knight brings action in a defending mode. He wants to help people, but gets so carried away that he misses the point. Does this sound like anyone you know?

Queen of Swords - The Queen is fair, just, and diplomatic. She cuts away things that are not appropriate with her sword. She speaks on behalf of others. She also wears a divorce bracelet (divorce from a person or situation).

King of Swords - The King is outspoken if he sees an injustice. He has strong beliefs of what's right and wrong. He can represent a judge or a policeman.

So You Wanna Read Tarot?

PENTACLES
* EARTH * SECURITY * ENERGY * MONEY *GROUNDING *

Page of Pentacles - The Page brings **news** about an opportunity for money or an offer of security in the form of words or a letter. You will be hearing of this soon.

Knight of Pentacles - Knights bring **change** – an offer of a security or energy, a job or a promotion is forthcoming. Be willing to act.

Queen of Pentacles - Queen represents a **secure** woman, someone who is very capable at home and in business. She may be a perfectionist. Is it someone you know?

King of Pentacles – The King represents an earthy, security-minded individual. He can represent a banker, businessman, investor, or someone who offers stability.

 **Try This:**

Make A Tarot Spinner

Make a copy of the astrological wheel shown in this chapter. Cut it out and paste it on a piece of poster board or card stock. Color it with colored pencils. Poke a hole in the center of the wheel with the tip of a scissor. From the left over poster board, cut out an arrow like this… . Poke a hole in the center of this arrow. Using a paper fastener put the tip of the fastener through the arrow first, then through the astrology wheel you have created. Fasten the ends behind the wheel by folding them outward. The arrow should spin freely.

Now you can make a game out of learning which Queen, King, or Page goes with which sign. Spin the arrow and see where it lands. Pull out the corresponding card from your deck. See if that card reminds you of the zodiac sign associated with it. Take notes in your journal. Spin again. Keep trying until you go through each card on the wheel. It's a fun way to learn.

Chapter 10

The Minors

The Minor Arcana are the cards that have numbers on them, with no titles. They are each part of the suit of wands, cups, swords or pentacles. There are a total of 56 cards in the Minor Arcana. In each suit there are 10 numbered cards and four court cards, namely the King, Queen, Knight and Page in each suit. These cards tell the story of the smaller things in life, the everyday events that happen daily.

One thing to remember when reading a Minor Arcana card is that the number tells you what action or struggle you are facing and the suit (wands, cups, swords or pentacles) tells you what area to focus on when interpreting it. Any symbols on the cards that you can interpret using what you have learned from the Major Arcana in the previous chapter can give you clues. When examining the card yourself, you tend to learn it better.

Definitions of the Numbers

If you follow these short definitions in order, you will see a pattern to them. It shows the pattern that a new project takes from start to finish like a cycle of life.

1's (Aces) – new beginnings, new opportunities, fresh starts

2's – the need for a decision, balance, patience

3's – groups, creativity, communications

4's – reason, authority, consolidation

5's – intuition, change, upset, adaptation

6's – harmony, choices, discrimination

7's – victory, challenges, test of faith

8's – power, success

9's – completion, fulfillment, the end

10's – rebirth, new start after completion

- *I always suggest looking at each minor card and read its meaning, aloud. Then study the picture on the card and see if the picture tells you that story.*

THE WANDS

Ace of Wands (1) *It's a fresh start in creativities or passions, new beginnings, or the creation of something new.*	**Six of Wands** A card of victory, you will be successful in what you are doing. You will be rewarded and come to a successful completion.
Two of Wands *Where do you go from here? This is a card of making plans with a couple of accomplishments already under your belt. It's time to decide what to do next.*	**Seven of Wands** It is a struggle to stay on top, but with your determination and courage you can overcome this.
Three of Wands *You finally see "your ship come in". Things are finally going to pan out. Success and completion is coming your way.*	**Eight of Wands** Right on target! Things will start happening now. There is no delay. It may happen all at once though.
Four of Wands *It's a celebration of harmony. You share this place with someone. Sometimes this is an event such as an engagement or some type of celebration.*	**Nine of Wands** You are on the defensive. It seems you have been there before. You will not let it happen again. You have your guard up.
Five of Wands *It shows competition and struggle. There may be some conflicts or squabbles which you will need to overcome.*	**Ten of Wands** You are carrying more than your fair share of the load. You need to delegate some of this. Lighten your load.

THE CUPS

Ace of Cups (1) Your emotions are overflowing with an abundance of love, luck and happiness. It can also mean a huge celebration, such as a wedding.	**Six of Cups** This is a card of friends and past acquaintances. Remember your past as it will help with your future.
Two of Cups It signifies the beginnings of a relationship. It represents that initial encounter- full of passion and understanding.	**Seven of Cups** There are too many possibilities. It seems you are scattered. Focus on one thing at a time and you will accomplish lots.
Three of Cups It stands for fun with friends. It's party-time! Celebrate with happiness. It's time to be around friends.	**Eight of Cups** You are searching for that missing piece of your life. Make a plan to find it and you will.
Four of Cups You need to look at what is being offered. Don't let chance pass you by. There are lots of possibilities, so look for them.	**Nine of Cups** Everything is going great. This is the happy-camper card. Victory and abundance is yours. Much success is evident.
Five of Cups Loss and regret surround you. You are upset over something, but remember, even though a few things went wrong, you still have a couple of good things behind you.	**Ten of Cups** This card represents family happiness and a secure life. Everything is perfect. Enjoy the peacefulness of your surroundings and a good family life.

THE SWORDS

Ace of Swords (1) It's a fresh start in action. It stands for making things happen. Victory will happen through strength and determination.	**Six of Swords** This card indicates travel or a move in a different direction or possibly to a harmonious location.
Two of Swords You are a little in the dark. You have to make a decision by yourself without any outside help.	**Seven of Swords** Be careful, something sneaky is going on. Watch your back. You are facing opposition.
Three of Swords This stands for heartache, major disappointment, conflict and sorrow. Something or someone is breaking your heart or you are breaking theirs.	**Eight of Swords** You are being tied up by your own thoughts. You are thinking things over too much. Sort out the details and don't dwell on them or you'll drive yourself crazy.
Four of Swords You need rest and relaxation. You need to take a break, go on vacation, and get away from it all to recuperate.	**Nine of Swords** It's the card of worry and despair. Something is causing you to worry. Don't panic. Have faith in yourself and use strength to proceed.
Five of Swords This is a *no-win* situation. Sometimes it can mean defeat. No matter what you do, you will not win. The matter is at a standstill.	**Ten of Swords** You're at a low point in your life, but it appears that the worst is over. Have hope, the sun is beginning to rise.

The PENTACLES

Ace of Pentacles (1) This card represents an offer of success. Money is coming your way. It can signify a new financial start. Take a risk!	**Six of Pentacles** There may be an unexpected gift of money. You will have much luck and success. Your generosity allows you to help others.
Two of Pentacles You need to make a decision to keep things in balance. You won't have to worry if you can keep things balanced.	**Seven of Pentacles** You are at a point where you are looking over what you have, kind of "taking inventory". More growth is coming, so don't stop now.
Three of Pentacles Some kind of skilled learning experience is coming (school, courses, business). Sometimes this card means you need counseling.	**Eight of Pentacles** You are skilled and hard-working. You keep going over things to perfect them. You will be rewarded for your hard work.
Four of Pentacles You like to hang on to what you've got. Sometimes this can make you ungiving. What's yours is yours and that's all there is to it!	**Nine of Pentacles** This signifies lots of prosperity. You are comfortable with all of your material possessions. You give excellent advice.
Five of Pentacles Difficult circumstances leave you feeling left out in the cold. Money problems have been surfacing. Don't worry though.	**Ten of Pentacles** You and your family are very secure and have prospered. You are very comfortable with your home life.

 Try This:

A Key Ring Memory Booster

Make a key ring to help you learn the Minor Arcana. Make a photocopy or trace the picture on each card - it works best on heavier paper like photo paper or flyer paper. Color in the picture with colored pencils, using the actual card as a sample. Punch a hole in the upper left corner of each card and clip them together with a round key ring. On the back of each card, write a few descriptive words that describe the card's meaning to you. You can use this to study from or to help you during your readings. It is a portable "cheat sheet". I once had a student take a fine line marker and write each card's meaning around the border of each actual card. She said this helped her greatly and soon she found herself not having to rely on the words anymore. After that she went out and bought a new clean deck.

D. L. Cocchio

Chapter 11

Reading Reversed Cards

~ As Blocked Energy ~

Some readers and occasional instruction manuals say that when a card turns up upside-down in a reading the meanings are reversed (totally opposite). Other manuals claim that it is more reliable to read the card as "the energy is blocked", and turn the card upright. First of all, some good advice is to make a mental note on which card it was. When you come to the spot in the reading that the card showed up "reversed", use your intuition or your gut feeling to see how you feel about it. Read the card the way that you feel is right. I have been taught both ways, but the "blocked energy" theory turns out to be true in most of the readings. When saying that the energy is blocked, you are merely saying that something is stopping that particular thing from happening. Together, you and the person you are reading can figure out how to unblock it, and figure out what they need to work on to make it happen the right way. This is a great "consulting" moment.

Deciding to Read a "Reversed Card"

If you decide you want to use a "reverse card" approach, here is a short list I've compiled from numerous other guides that may help you.

Reversed – Wands

Ace of Wands – You are stuck, lack of money, blocks your progress
Two of Wands - Loss of interest, nothing happening
Three of Wands – Unclear goals, lack of resources
Four of Wands – Celebrations, delayed lack of support
Five of Wands – New business opportunities
Six of Wands – Losers, delay
Seven of Wands – Being shamed, embarrassed
Eight of Wands – Jealousy, going nowhere fast
Nine of Wands – Unaware of dangers
Ten of Wands – Expecting too much of yourself
Page of Wands – Unpleasant news, can't decide
Knight of Wands – Interruption
Queen of Wands – opposition, jealousy
King of Wands – quarrel or opposition

Reversed – Cups

Ace of Cups – Loss from what you love
Two of Cups – Misunderstandings, broken promises
Three of Cups – Social event delayed
Four of Cups – New opportunities
Five of Cups – Hopeful expectations, good news
Six of Cups – Living in the past
Seven of Cups – Make up your mind
Eight of Cups – Getting things moving
Nine of Cups – Mistakes made
Ten of Cups – Without friendship or support
Page of Cups – Subconscious obstacles
Knight of Cups - Trickery
Queen of Cups - Dishonesty
King of Cups – Loss or scandal

Reversed – Swords

Ace of Swords – Too much power leads to disaster
Two of Swords – Action is taken for release
Three of Swords – Disorder, confusion, stress
Four of Swords – Get back to action
Five of Swords – Weakness, defeat
Six of Swords – No way out, stalemate
Seven of Swords – Good advice, getting it together
Eight of Swords - Freedom
Nine of Swords – Light at the end of the tunnel
Ten of Swords – Get on with your life
Page of Swords – Unforeseen events
Knight of Swords – A sudden departure
Queen of Swords - Manipulation
King of Swords – Cruelty, unjust actions

Reversed – Pentacles

Ace of Pentacles – It's hard to get going, money delays
Two of Pentacles – Lack of balance
Three of Pentacles – Lack of skill
Four of Pentacles – You can let it go
Five of Pentacles – End of hard times
Six of Pentacles – Unfairness in business
Seven of Pentacles – Financial difficulty
Eight of Pentacles – Inattention to detail
Nine of Pentacles – Shaky finances, frustration
Ten of Pentacles – Family fights, burdened by family
Page of Pentacles – Bad news, problems
Knight of Pentacles – Careless habits, money loss
Queen of Pentacles – Reckless with money
King of Pentacles – Greedy, unreliable

Reversed – Major Arcana

The Fool – A faulty choice
Magician - Indecision
High Priestess –Accepting surface knowledge
Empress – Neglecting your health & body
Emperor – Emotional immaturity
Hierophant -Unconventional
Lovers – An unwise choice
Chariot – Pulled in two directions at once
Strength – Pay attention to your own needs
Hermit – You are staying busy to avoid what you need to deal with.

So You Wanna Read Tarot?

Wheel of Fortune – You will reap what you have sown.
Justice – Delays in legal matters
Hanged Man – You can't seem to move forward
Death – Confront your fears, stagnation
Temperance – You are out of balance
Devil – Potential for things to go wrong
Tower – An accident waiting to happen
Star – Blocked from your goals, doubt
Moon – Your daily demands are overwhelming.
Sun – Future plans are clouded
Judgement – You need to face reality.
World – Fear of change

D. L. Cocchio

Chapter 12

Astrology Fun

The tarot cards are also linked to astrology. Sometimes the aspects or traits of the astrological sign associated with a particular card will have an impact on how to read the card. It will give you more insight as to the aspects associated with that card.

This also gives you yet another clue into determining the meaning of the card. Some of the cards are also linked to an astrological planet. If you want, you can associate a friend or family member whose zodiac sign matches the one tied to a card. You may find that the particular person has many of those traits and can embody the meaning of the card for you.

Astrological Signs of the Zodiac

Capricorn (the goat)	Dec. 22 – Jan. 19
Aquarius (the water-bearer)	Jan. 20 – Feb. 18
Pisces (the fishes)	Feb. 19 – Mar. 20
Aries (the ram)	Mar. 21 – Apr. 19
Taurus (the bull)	Apr. 20 – May 20
Gemini (the twins)	May 21 – Jun. 21
Cancer (the crab)	Jun. 22 – Jul. 22
Leo (the lion)	Jul. 23 – Aug. 22
Virgo (the maiden)	Aug. 23 – Sept. 22
Libra (the scales)	Sept. 23 – Oct. 22
Scorpio (the scorpion)	Oct. 23 – Nov. 21
Sagittarius (the archer)	Nov. 22 – Dec. 21

So You Wanna Read Tarot?

CARDS & PLANETS

MAJOR ARCANA TAROT CARD	**SIGN OR PLANET**
The Fool	Uranus
The Magician	Mercury
The High Priestess	Moon
The Empress	Venus
The Emperor	Aries
The Hierophant	Taurus
The Lovers	Gemini
The Chariot	Cancer
Strength	Leo
The Hermit	Virgo
The Wheel of Fortune	Jupiter
Justice	Libra
The Hanged Man	Neptune
Death	Scorpio
Temperance	Sagittarius
The Devil	Capricorn
The Tower	Mars
The Star	Aquarius
The Moon	Pisces
The Sun	Sun
Judgement	Pluto
The World	Saturn

Traits of Each Astrological Sign

Capricorn - Capricorns are very responsible, careful, patient and determined. They use brains instead of force, and are quick to seize an opportunity. Capricorns' most likeable trait is their steadiness. They are ambitious and are motivated by a desire for success, status and money. Most seek leadership and power. You can count on a Capricorn. People enjoy their strong sense of humor. Capricorns will not forgive anyone that belittles them. They can be control-freaks, at times. A Capricorn is usually a loner.

Aquarius - Aquarians are independent, assertive, and have strong opinions about things. They have a tendency to get into unusual situations and have unusual friends. Aquarians are very friendly and are people-oriented. They don't care what other people think. Being open-minded, they are seekers of knowledge and are concerned with the welfare of the world. Keeping their distance, Aquarians try not to get involved in intimate relationships. Aquarians are also creative, imaginative, and love to experiment. They are determined to not be like everyone else. Aquarians can change people's lives for the better just by being around. They always see to it that everybody is happy. Their most likeable qualities are being easygoing, kind, honest, helpful and never boring.

Pisces - Pisceans are mystical, intuitive, emotional, imaginative, receptive, and romantic. They are easily drawn into bad situations and are drawn to unbalanced people. They are compassionate, adaptable, and are greatly influenced by their surroundings. Pisces have the gift of prophecy and should use it by trusting their intuition. They prefer to work alone. They need to learn to say no. Pisceans usually have a pleasant personality and are loyal, caring, sentimental, unselfish and generous. They make great friends.

Aries - Aries are courageous and like to be independent. It is an active, energetic, excitable, impulsive, optimistic, and creative sign. Aries is open to change and new experiences. They are also prone to accidents and tend to get into dangerous situations. They've earned a reputation for not finishing what they have started. Aries are lucky with money, but can't hold on to it. Aries is a "me-first" sign.

Taurus - Taureans are quiet, affectionate and patient people. They are determined, very stubborn, and resistant to change. A Taurean cannot rush into anything new. A love of material things such as money and possessions is important to them. They look for permanency, grounding and stability. Taurus people are sensuous, sentimental, and very down-to-earth. They make great friends.

Gemini - Gemini is a sign of thought and communication. Geminis are lively, energetic, and intellectual. They adapt to new situations, easily. Their most likeable trait is their responsiveness. Gemini have a restless nature, are quick in thought and action, and are always on the go. Disliking routine and monotony, they like freedom and change. Geminis have the gift of persuasion and can have a dual personality.

Cancer - Cancer people are very sensitive, sympathetic, kind and emotional. They are imaginative, receptive, temperamental, and unpredictable. They need encouragement and approval. Cancers keep things inside and like to sulk when offended. They have a heart of gold. Cancereans are very moody people, one minute appearing gentle, kind and sympathetic, and the next, cranky and snapping at everyone and everything. Their most likeable trait is loyalty.

Leo - Leos are enthusiastic, generous, creative and powerful. They are very fixed in their opinion. Leos are devoted to themselves and do things in a really big way. They are kind and openhearted. Nobody could ask for a better friend. Flattery will get you everywhere with a Leo. They thrive on it. Leos can be overbearing at times, but their bark is worse than their bite.

Virgo - Virgos are reserved, analytical, modest, and practical. They seek to know and understand things. Virgos are very conscientious and intelligent. They have excellent memory and clear thinking. Virgos tend to complicate things. They tend to interfere with their own criticism and can be hypercritical. They can also be shy and reserved. Money matters a lot to a Virgo.

Libra - Libras are easily liked. They are good listeners. They are active, artistic, easy-going and sociable. Libras like balance and harmony and are happiest when things are in order. They have a tendency to stir people up with their being very fickle. Libras tend to judge others by their appearance. Money tends to slip through their fingers easily and they love elegance. They dislike hard work. They are very romantic and their most likeable trait is their charm. Libras do everything in their power to please people.

Scorpio - Scorpios are imaginative, passionate, emotional, unpredictable, adaptable, intense and persistent. They are secretive and can be very jealous. Scorpios can have sharp stinging tempers and can enrage others. They have a complex mind and can also be very intense. Relationships are usually complicated for a Scorpio. Scorpions are deeply loyal to their friends. They tend to become obsessive and passionate in whatever they become involved with. With a Scorpio - it is either all or nothing. Scorpio people never forget a kindness, but can never forgive when they get hurt.

Sagittarius - Sagittarians are ambitious, energetic, optimistic, and generous. They like challenge, and like to explore. They have a strong desire for freedom and are a free, adventurous spirit. Sometimes they are too interested in what will happen tomorrow to worry about what went wrong today. Sagittarians are kind, always helping, have a good sense of humor, are great communicators, imaginative, clever and honest. What they say is what they mean. They are very likeable, but have a problem finishing what they start.

D. L. Cocchio

Chapter 13

Are You Ready?

You may want to start off by reading for yourself at first. It is great practice and helps you to become familiar with cards in the beginning. When you are comfortable with reading for yourself, try practicing on a friend. The instructions below will give you guidelines when reading with your friend. When you read for yourself, just pretend that you are in her place.

When your friend arrives, your main job is to make her feel relaxed and at ease. Many times the person has never had their cards read before and may be afraid that they might hear something bad. You, as the reader, must help to put their mind at rest.

A few minutes of chatting with the person is a good icebreaker. It helps the person to feel more at ease. Next, explain that you will shuffle the deck to clear it of vibrations from your last reading. Also, by shuffling in front of your friend, you can demonstrate several ways to shuffle.

D. L. Cocchio

Which spread is best?

Now you need to determine which is the best spread for that particular reading. A spread is the pattern that you use to lay the cards out in. There are many different spreads available to use. First, ask if they have any questions or if they want you to concentrate on any one subject in particular. Then, you can figure out which spread to use based on the questions.

The Celtic Spread is a good one for giving you a lot of information about a topic. It tells you the present, past, and future. It also shows you hopes and fears, blockages, your environment, and what the result will be, provided that you stay on that course. You will be taught this spread later in the book.

The Three Card Spread is good for a quick reading on one particular subject. It shows you how the problem started, what you can do about it, and what the result will be. It can also give you information on the past, present and future status of a problem. The information is very limited, but a great time saver and good for a quick answer.

The Astrology Spread is good for learning a little about each area in a person's life. It tells about past, money, communications, romance, endings and beginnings, travel, education, home, creativity, children, work, friendships, and emotions. This is a great spread to use when your friend has no particular question.

Since most of you are just beginning as tarot readers, I would suggest starting out with The Three Card Spread or The Celtic Cross Spread until you are very comfortable with it, then branch out and try other spreads. You can find other spreads

So You Wanna Read Tarot?

in a later chapter in this book. Always try a spread on yourself first, so that you can become familiar with it before trying it one someone else. The Celtic-Cross Spread is a favorite because it gives you a lot of information in one reading.

 Try This:

A Boyfriend or Girlfriend Quickie Question

Think of a boyfriend or girlfriend question and shuffle the cards. When you feel they are fully shuffled, stop. Cut the deck into 3 piles and flip the top card of each pile. This is The Three Card Spread. Reading left to right, the first pile shows you how the situation started. The second pile tells you what can be done about it. And the third pile tells you what is most likely to happen with him if you take that advice. Look up each card meaning in this book. See how you do with this short reading.

Things To Remember

- Don't smoke, drink, or have loud music. All of this is distracting and you need to be focused.

- Incense is a nice touch, but make sure that your friend or the person you are reading for isn't allergic to it.

- If at all possible, the reader should sit at the North side of the table, facing South and the person you are reading for should sit opposite you because the magnetic energy flows North and South. Again, if this is not possible, it is okay. It's just a suggestion.

- Make the person you are reading for feel at ease by chatting a little bit first before the reading.

So You Wanna Read Tarot?

Chapter 14

Shuffle Those Cards!

These are step-by-step instructions to read for your friend. Please try this method out on yourself first. Do some self-discovery and ask yourself questions such as "What do I need to know in this situation?", "What is my next step?" or "What will I be when I grow up?"

Step 1: First, your friend should sit directly across from you. The candles should already be lit and your crystal (if you choose to have one) should be near you.

Step 2: Shuffle the cards a few times then hand them to your friend. Ask her to shuffle the cards while thinking of a particular question or subject. If she can't narrow it down, tell her to concentrate on life in general for a period of the next few months. When she feels that she is done shuffling, have her place the cards in one pile in front of you.

Step 3: While the friend is shuffling, you could take this opportunity to calm yourself and close your eyes. Relax after a tough day at school or work. Tell the person that you are just going to close your eyes for a moment to clear your mind. This way they don't question your actions. With your eyes closed, take this moment to ask your spirit guides or God "to circle us in the white light for protection and to protect us from any and all negativity stemming from the past, the present, or the future". At this time ask (in your mind, of course) "if any spirit has a message that they want me to pass on?" Be quiet for a minute and see if you hear anything back in response. If you don't, it's okay, but you may hear an answer in the very near future.

Step 4: Next, open your eyes (welcome back!). Ask your friend to separate the pile in front of her into three piles, taking notice of which pile came from the top of the deck and which came from the bottom. Now, pick up the piles one at a time by choosing the pile that came from the bottom of the deck first. This becomes the top of your new pile. Pick up the remaining two piles in reverse order. This is just a good way of cutting the deck.

Step 5: Lay out your cards so that they are facing you, the reader. If the first card is reversed or upside down you should turn the whole deck around to correct the situation. Try not to make faces as you turn them over. Always mention that the Death card rarely means the death of a person, that it usually means transformation or death of a situation.

You know the saying - "out with the old and in with the new". This way the other person doesn't panic or become afraid if that card shows up.

Step 6: If you begin using the Three-Card Spread, you don't even have to pick up the piles. You can leave the piles the way the client put them down. Flip over the top card of each pile. Turn the card so it faces you.

D. L. Cocchio

THREE CARD SPREAD

The **left** pile represents the *past or what caused the situation*.

The **middle** pile represents *what can be done about it.*

The **right pile** represents the *future* and *what will happen if you do what the middle pile said to do.*

Left Pile (PAST)	Middle Pile (PRESENT)	Right Pile (FUTURE)

>  **Try This:**
>
> ## Make A Layout Map
>
> Using a piece of poster board, draw a layout of the Celtic Cross Spread, shown to you on the next page in this chapter. Trace the outline of a card for each position in the layout. Underneath each card position write a few words to describe what the position tells about. This will be your "teaching map" to help out while you are learning. You'll find it will make your learning a little bit easier. You can use the template while you are trying to learn the cards. This way there is no need to learn two different things at once - the cards and the spreads. Eventually you will find that you won't need to rely on the map anymore.

*A note about the **Celtic Cross Spread** on the next page. – Upon researching, I found out that there are several different ways to lay out the Celtic Cross. The following is the way that is most well - known and the way that I was taught to lay it out.*

THE CELTIC CROSS SPREAD

If you prefer, you can use this pattern to lay out your cards. Lay the cards in the order of the numbers according to the diagram.

```
                    ┌─────────┐
                    │   5     │              ┌─────────┐
                    │  What   │              │   10    │
                    │ Helps or│              │  Final  │
                    │  Hurts  │              │ Outcome │
                    │   You   │              └─────────┘
                    └─────────┘
                    ┌─────────┐              ┌─────────┐
                    │   1     │              │   9     │
                    │ What's  │              │  Your   │
                    │ Up Now  │              │  Hopes  │
┌─────┐             └─────────┘   ┌─────┐    └─────────┘
│  4  │             ┌─────────┐   │  6  │    ┌─────────┐
│ The │             │   2     │   │What's│   │   8     │
│ Past│             │What Gets│   │Coming│   │ Other's │
│     │             │In The Way│  │  Up  │   │Feelings │
└─────┘             └─────────┘   └─────┘    └─────────┘
                    ┌─────────┐              ┌─────────┐
                    │   3     │              │   7     │
                    │  Basis  │              │Negative │
                    │   Of    │              │Feelings │
                    │Question │              │ (fears) │
                    └─────────┘              └─────────┘
```

1. **What's Happening Now** – The feeling of the situation. What's going on right now.

2. **What Gets In The Way** – What you're up against.

3. **Basis of Situation** – The real reason you are asking the question.

4. **The Past** – What's led up to the present situation?

5. **What Helps or Hurts You** – What will help or hurt you in getting the desired result.

6. **What's Coming Up** – The most likely thing to happen next.

7. **Negative Feelings** – Your fears and negative attitudes.

8. **Other's Feelings** – How others around you feel about the situation (your environment).

9. **Hopes** – This represents what you are hoping for.

10. **Final Outcome** – The result, provided nothing changes.

Spread out the remaining cards by fanning them out across the bottom of your table right in front of you. You can pull cards from here for more verification, as needed.

Here's a handy worksheet for you to use in the beginning...

 ## Tarot Worksheet

Card Position	Card Pulled	What It Means
1. What's Happening Now		
2. What Gets In The Way		
3. Basis of Situation		
4. The Past		
5. What Helps or Hurts You		
6. What's Coming		
7. Negative Feelings/ Fears		
8. Other's Feelings		
9. Your Hopes		
10. Final Outcome		

Chapter 15

Think Before You Speak

Before you blurt out anything, take a moment and look at the card spread as a whole. You don't want to put your foot in your mouth!

<u>Look at the suits...</u>

Are there mostly cups? If so, your reading will focus mostly on emotions or love.

Are there mostly swords? If so, your reading will focus mostly on communication, ideas or struggles.

Are there mostly wands? If so, your reading will focus mostly on self, your passions, or creativity.

Are there mostly pentacles? If so, your reading will focus mostly on money, security, or energy.

<u>Look at the repeated numbers...</u>

This gives you an idea of where the reading is heading. If you follow the short definitions in order, you will see a pattern to them. It shows the pattern that a new project takes from start to finish like a cycle of life.

"Think of them, as the steps taken towards success."

    1's (Aces) – new beginnings, new opportun-ities, fresh starts

    2's – the need for a decision, balance, patience

    3's – groups, creativity, communications

    4's – reason, authority, consolidation

    5's – intuition, change, upset, adaptation

    6's – harmony, choices, discrimination

    7's – victory, challenges, test of faith

    8's – power, success

    9's – completion, fulfillment, the end

    10's – rebirth, new start after completion

Practice by taking each suit and laying them out in front of you, one suit at a time, in the numbered order starting with Aces, twos, threes, etc. Look at the meanings and compare the cards. Check the pictures and the guide words. See how the picture illustrates the words associated with the number on the card. This will help you visualize the meanings.

So You Wanna Read Tarot?

Smart Tips:

- **Tip 1:** The position that the card is in could change the meaning slightly. Look at the cards surrounding it and blend it with their meanings.

- **Tip 2:** If your intuition tells you *not* to say something - then don't.

- **Tip 3:** If you see something terrible, remember this – you can't drop a bombshell of terrible news in a 15-minute reading and expect the person to deal with it. Instead, give the person advice to steer them in a direction that may change the problem. An example would be to suggest that it is time to make that doctor's appointment (for health problems).

- **Tip 4:** <u>No</u> alcohol or caffeine when reading cards, you want to remain a clear channel. Stick to water!

- **Tip 5:** A card has many meanings; always talk about the symbols that your eyes focus on first.

- **Tip 6:** Are you picking up any intuitive messages?

- **Tip 7:** Always read for the best of all concerned and to cause no harm.

- **Tip 8:** Keeping things confidential is a must!

- **Tip 9:** Predicting fatal accidents, death, etc. is harmful. Instead, give them suggestions that would steer them away from such an event.

- **Tip 10:** Trust your answers the first time. Do not ask the same question over and over again.

- **Tip 11:** Try to keep your opinions out of the reading.

- **Tip 12:** Practice on yourself before trying things out on a friend.

Frequently Asked Questions

Question 1 - *There are so many meanings for one card. How do I know which meaning I should talk about?*

When reading a card, talk about the first thing that your eyes focus on. If that happens to be what the character is holding, then interpret that symbol first. See how that ties into your reading. You can also ask the person what subject they were concentrating on when they shuffled the cards in order to give you a clue of where to start.

Question 2 – *What if I am drawing a blank and nothing is coming to mind?*

Don't panic if you are drawing a blank. You can always refer to this book to help out. In the beginning you will want to look up each card in the book to see what it is all about. If the entire spread overwhelms you, just focus on the first two cards. See what the first card means and how it relates to the subject. Then see what the second card means and how it relates. Next, combine the two meanings. Let your intuition come into play here and see what comes to mind. Then go to the third card, look it up and try to tie the meaning into the subject at hand. How does this relate to the first two cards?

Does it change the meaning at all? The cards tell a story, so try to put the story together for your friend. Tarot cards are like pieces to a puzzle, and as the reader, it is your job to put the puzzle together and make sense of it. If you are stuck on a card, feel free to draw another card from the leftover pile to clarify the meaning and see if the new card sheds some light on the subject. With patience and perseverance this will all eventually become routine. Like they say – practice makes perfect.

Question 3 – *What if my reading isn't making sense?*

If you've gone over it several times and the reading just isn't making sense, then gather up the cards, reshuffle, and try a different spread. If that doesn't work out either, then tell your friend that the cards do not want to tell her the answer right now about that subject. Sometimes it's not in our best interest to know the outcome of a situation before we experience it. There are times that we must experience it for ourselves and try not to change our fate because of an important lesson we need to learn in there somewhere. Then have her ask a different question for now.

Question 4 – *What if I have a nagging thought in my head and I can't shake it?*

At this point I would like to take a moment to mention errant thoughts that may pop into your head during a reading. Sometimes a nagging thought may consume you and I have learned over the years that you should say it aloud because, as silly as it may seem, it may be a clue that the client will recognize. Here's one example: During one reading I kept hearing the Disney theme song from the popular movie,

Beauty and the Beast. So I said to my client, "This may sound silly to you, but I am hearing the song from *Beauty and the Beast* over and over again. I can't shake it. Does it mean anything to you?" Her eyes welled up with tears and she could barely choke back her response, "Oh my God, my grandpa used to always call me "Beauty" when I was little. It was his pet name for me. And I was hoping to hear something about my Grandpa during this reading. In fact I asked him for a sign and there it is. Thank you so, so much!"

So, as silly as it may seem, talk out loud about anything you are hearing or seeing. Share it with your client because it just may be what they were looking for.

 Try This:

Make a Handy Cheat Sheet

Take an index card and write the numbers 1 to 10 down in a column. After each number, write a few words describing each number as shown. Use this card as a quick reference and keep it with your tarot deck when you read. After a while you won't even need to refer to it anymore. Yay!

Chapter 16

Can We Play Games?

Game #1 - The Fortune Cookie Game

Did you ever hear of the game that people sometimes play when they are eating fortune cookies with a group of friends? Well, the way the game goes is that everyone takes a fortune cookie and each friend opens their cookie one at a time, reading it aloud to the group. At the end of every fortune that is read, the reader must say "in love", which relates all of the messages of fortune to one topic – love.

Well, the reason I'm telling you about this in the first place is because if you make a game out of tarot reading, sometimes it helps you to relate to the topic at hand. It's fun to try to use this idea of the "Fortune Cookie Game" and incorporate it into your card readings. An example would be: when trying to concentrate on the topic of money or finances when reading a card's meaning, say "in money matters" after you tell the card's meaning. If the card of XIV – Temperance comes up in this instance, you might say that it indicates that moderation and balance is needed, be patient and take little baby-steps **"in matters of money"**.

You will find that this little game may help you to tie the cards in to focusing on the topic better. Have fun and experiment!

Game #2 - The Daily Fortune Game

Another game you can play is a daily game to find out more about yourself and your life. Every morning before school or work, spend about 5-10 minutes by yourself in a quiet spot with your cards. Shuffle your cards and ask aloud "Tell me what to expect today". Pull out one card from the deck and focus on it. What symbols do your eyes focus on first? What is the meaning of the card? Look it up if you need to. How does this relate to your daily activity? Jot down a couple of notes in a diary before leaving the house. You can refer to this later on and compare your activities to what was predicted. After doing this for several weeks, you begin to understand the cards better.

Game #3 – The "What's Up?" Game

This is a great game for a group of friends. If you are having a party or the gang over, try out this game. After shuffling the deck of cards, fan them out, face down in your hands. Go around the room and have each friend concentrate on a subject and select a card, but tell them not to turn it over just yet. When everyone has chosen a card, put the pile aside and ask each friend, one at a time, to reveal her card and tell you what subject they were concentrating on. Now use your intuition, this book, or a cheat sheet to tell them about the card, tying it into their subject. Congratulations, you just gave them a short reading! Good job!

Game #4 – The Visualization Game

This game is to be played alone. It is a visualization game that will help you to meditate on each card for a deeper understanding of the meaning of each card. I would choose to play this game with the Major Arcana Cards only (the ones with the Roman Numerals on them). This is how it was taught in a class I attended.

Step 1: First, pick out your favorite Major Arcana Card.

Step 2: Look at the card, study it and try to remember exactly what it looks like.

Step 3: Close your eyes and try to picture the card in front of you, recalling the details that you studied.

Step 4: Open your eyes and look at the card again to see what you left out. Also look at the colors, backgrounds, placement and objects.

Step 5: Close your eyes again and see how much more you can picture. After several tries you will get it right.

Step 6: Finally, relax, sit back in your chair, and close your eyes. Now meditate and use your imagination to visualize the card in your mind once again.

Step 7: In your mind see that card expanding to the size of a big picture window (from floor-to-ceiling)in front of you.

Step 8: See yourself stepping into this card by stepping through this window.

Step 9: Look around at the scenery and the landscape to the left and to the right. What do you see? What do you hear? Do you smell anything? What's the weather like? Make a mental note of it. You can touch things too. Experience the card. (Like virtual reality)

Step 10: Are there any figures in the picture with you? Are there any people or animals? Walk up to the thing that interests you the most. Ask the figure if he or she has a message or a gift for you. Ask what the gift is and what it is to be used for. Be sure to thank the figure. Ask any questions that you might have at this time. Listen for answers.

So You Wanna Read Tarot?

Step 11: Now it's time to go. Say goodbye and step out of the picture, back to the room. See the card shrinking back to normal size in front of you.

Step 12: Get a piece of paper or your notebook journal and write down everything that you experienced.

NOTE: If it helps, you can tape this visualization meditation on a cassette tape by reading the script aloud slowly, then you can play it back and follow along as it guides you.

> ❖ *It may seem like you are making it all up, but that's okay. It helps you to use your imagination and intuition. Be patient. They say that imagination is the key to all things. You will find out that it truly is!*

Chapter 17

Popular Tarot Card Spreads

In this chapter you will find Tarot spreads that are popular with young adults today. They cover topics such as boyfriends, best friends, soul mates, money, pets, careers, love and lust, home, school, family and friends. Each spread can be customized slightly to your purpose at hand. If the questions that are answered are similar to the questions that you seek, you can change the main topic by focusing on the topic that you are interested in while you are shuffling the cards. Most times it makes no difference because your intent while you are shuffling is what comes up in the cards. Your spirit guides know what you are looking for and will work with you. Give these spreads a try and see how much fun you can have for you and your friends!

D. L. Cocchio

15 Popular Spreads For Different Occasions

    I.   New Boyfriend or Girlfriend Spread

    II.   The Love Spread

    III.   "It's My Life" Spread

    IV.   All About My Pet Spread

    V.   The B - Day Spread (Birthday)

    VI.   The "What's Up?" Spread

    VII.   The Time Line Pyramid

    VIII.   Lucky Numbers Spread

    IX.   What Will I Be?

    X.   A Quick Answer To My Problem

    XI.   What About The Money?

    XII.   The Week Ahead Spread

    XIII.   Astrological Spread

    XIV.   Best Friends Spread

I. <u>New Boyfriend or Girlfriend Spread</u>

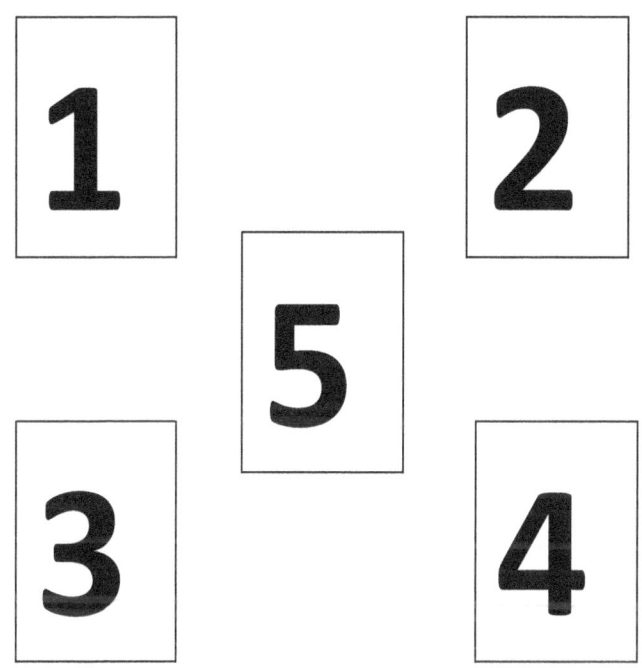

1). What do **you** bring to the relationship?

2). What does **the new boyfriend or girlfriend** bring to the relationship?

3). Will **you** be happy?

4). Will **he or she** be happy?

5.) Will **it** last?

II. The Love Spread

1). Your past love experience
2). Your current love experience
3). What you want
4). What you need
5). What you have to give
6). Your future love experience?

So You Wanna Read Tarot?

III. "IT'S MY LIFE" SPREAD

1). Home

2). School

3). Family

4). Friends

5). What you like to do now

6). What the future holds (career?)

7). What can help you get this

IV. All About My Pet Spread

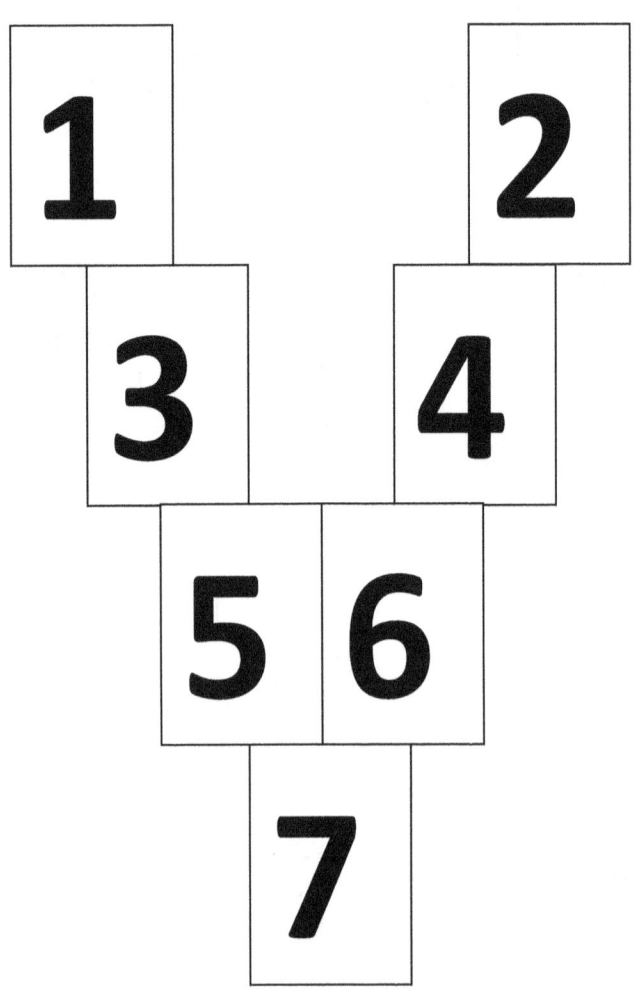

1). What your pet needs you to know

2). Your pet's feelings

3). What you can do to help

4). What your pet needs

5). Your pet's health

6). Your pet's future needs

7). What's in store for your pet

V. The BD Spread

(Birthday)

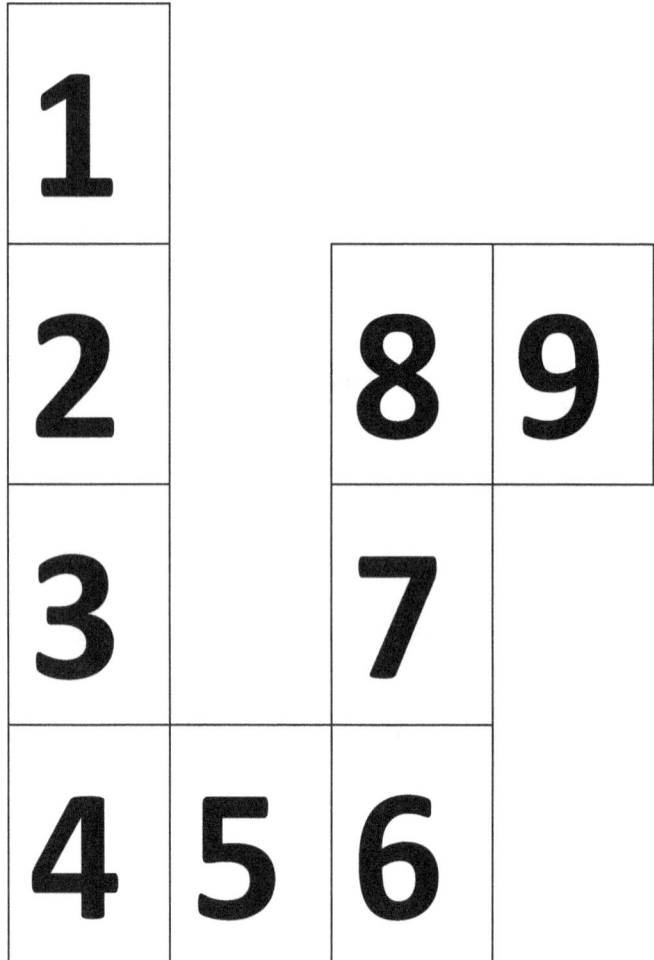

1). Where you are

2). Where you want to be on your birthday

3). What fuels your fire

4). What you need to do

5). The things you have done

6). The things you feel (emotions)

7). Your spirituality

8). What stands in your way

9). What to do to make your wish come true.

VI. THE "WHAT'S UP?" SPREAD

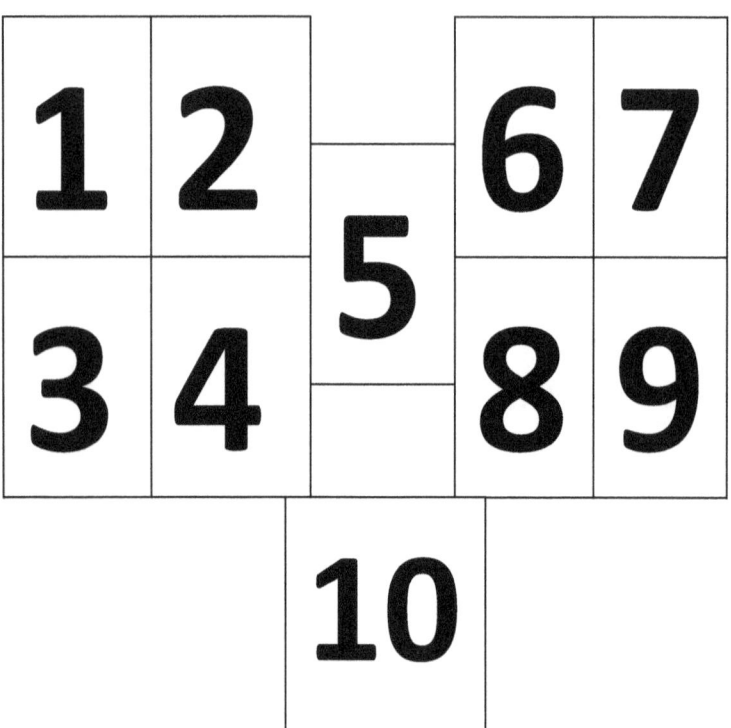

1-2). What's going on right now

3-4). Events coming up that will affect things

5). Where you are headed

6-7). What will happen if things stay the same

8-9). How you can change things

10). The outcome after the changes

VII. THE TIME LINE PYRAMID

What will happen in 9-12 months ....

10

In 6-9 months

8 **9**

In 3-6 mos.

5 **6** **7**

1 **2** **3** **4**

(Now) ♥ Read each line going across for what will happen during the corresponding times.

VIII. LUCKY NUMBERS SPREAD

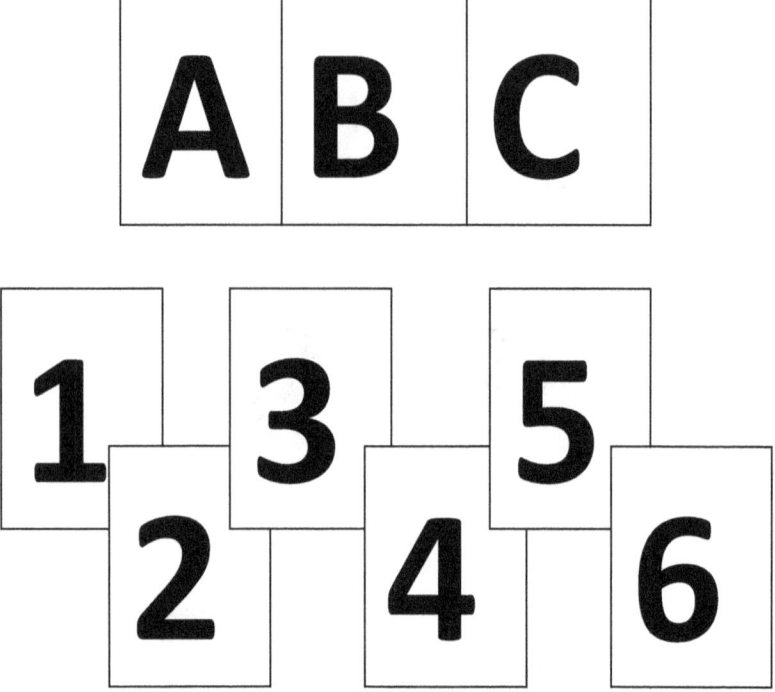

A. Should I buy a lottery ticket today?

B. Any obstacles for me?

C. What am I thinking about this?

Cards 1 – 6 : Use the numbers that turn up here to play the lottery.

Note: To play the numbers, just use the **numbered** cards in your deck for cards in positions 1 to 6.

IX. WHAT WILL I BE?

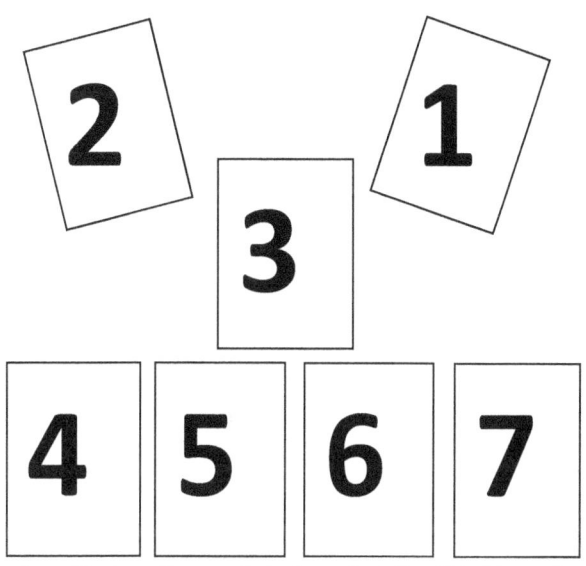

1. Do I really want to be what I'm thinking of being when I get older?

2. Tell me more about my possible profession.

3. What am I not able to change about my choice?

4. Am I doing my best?

5. What change can I make to help my choice along?

6. What is affecting my choices now?

7. What will be the outcome?

X. A Quick Answer To My Problem

[1] [2] [3]

1.) The nature of the problem

2.) What to do about the problem

3.) The answer – what will happen if you take the advice

XI. <u>What About The Money?</u>

1.) Your finances

2.) Money coming soon

3.) Money opportunities to check out

4.) What will bring the money or how will you get it?

5.) The end result

XII. THE WEEK AHEAD SPREAD

1	2	3
	4	
5	6	7

1.) Day One   5.) Day Five

2.) Day Two   6.) Day Six

3.) Day Three   7.) Day Seven

4.) Day Four

So You Wanna Read Tarot?

XIII. ASTROLOGICAL SPREAD

Shuffle and lay the first 12 cards out in a fanned circle like above. Each card will fall in a numbered space. Try to connect each card's meaning with the topic shown in the space that the card lands in.

This one is fun!

XIV. BEST FRIENDS SPREAD

1

2	3

4	5	6

7	8	9	10

So You Wanna Read Tarot?

Think of a friend while shuffling.

1. Past history of this friendship

2. Your past experience

3. Your friend's past experience

4. Your current experience

5. Your friend's current experience

6. The present relationship

7. What you may experience in the future

8. What your friend may experience

9. Where the friendship is headed

10. Future outcome – best friends forever?

D. L. Cocchio

Tarot Map –
The Spiritual Journey of the Soul
(each card leads to the next in your spiritual sequence)

0 - The Fool (beginning & innocence) ▶
I - The Magician (will, focus & desire) ▶
II – High Priestess (understanding & commitment) ▶
III – The Empress (creative imagination & growth) ▶
IV – The Emperor (reason, vision, stability & authority) ▶
V – The Hierophant (using traditional, established values) ▶
VI – Lovers (choices with confidence & harmony) ▶
VII – The Chariot (controlling senses, being in charge) ▶
VIII – Strength (courage & conviction) ▶
IX – The Hermit (self-discovery through inner reflection) ▶
X – Wheel of Fortune (change happening, already put in motion) ▶
XI – Justice (balance & effect) ▶
XII – The Hanged Man (pause now, take action later) ▶
XIII – Death (transformation & regeneration) ▶
XIV – Temperance (patience & moderation) ▶
XV – The Devil (bad habits, your downfall, material things that bind) ▶
XVI – The Tower (disruption & change) ▶
XVII – The Star (your hopes, dreams, & faith) ▶
XVII – The Moon (dangers & hidden things that surface) ▶
XIX – The Sun (extreme happiness & satisfaction) ▶
XX – Judgement (an awakening & leap of faith) ▶
XXI – The World (success & promises assured)

*Lay your cards out in order and follow the sequence to view the story they tell.

Chapter 18

The Cheat Sheets

This chapter contains "cheat sheets" containing lists of the Four suits, the Major Arcana, the Minor Arcana, the Court Cards and the remaining numbered cards. These sheets have short keys words and phrases to help you remember each card. They can come in handy when beginning to read. They are easy-to-read reference sheets to keep on hand when you are reading.

D. L. Cocchio

CHEAT SHEET OF THE FOUR SUITS

	Wands	Cups	Swords	Pentacles
Playing Card	Clubs	Hearts	Spades	Diamonds
Season:	Summer	Spring	Fall	Winter
Element:	Fire	Water	Air	Earth
Type of World:	Spiritual World	Emotional World	Mental World	Material World
Focus:	New Beginnings	Emotions	Communications	Money
Key Words:	Business, Creative, Passions, Desires	Artistic, Emotions, Nurturing, Intuition	Ideas, Action, Communication, Ideas, thoughts, Struggle	Energy, Security, Money, Grounding
Astrology:	Sagittarius, Aries, Leo	Scorpio, Cancer, Pisces	Gemini, Libra, Aquarius	Taurus, Capricorn, Virgo
Court Card represents a person with these traits:	Red/ fair hair, Blue eyes, Fair skin	Light brown hair, Blue/hazel eyes, Fair/med skin	Brown/ blk hair, Dark eyes, Med./dk. Skin	White/ Dark hair, Fair or Dark skin

So You Wanna Read Tarot?

Cheat Sheet Of The Major Arcana - Key Words

0 – The Fool	I – The Magician	II – The High Priestess
Fresh start	Will	Listen to intuition
New outlook	Energy	Commitment
Pay attention	Apply yourself	Knowledge
Carefree attitude	Make magic	Wisdom
Taking risks	Focus	Secrets
Adventurous	Desire	Pay attention
III – The Empress	**IV – The Emperor**	**V – The Hierophant**
Creativity	Father figure	Tradition
Motherhood	Authority	Religion
Fertility	Power	Have faith!
Femininity	Follow rules	Believe
Growth	The boss	Values
Abundance	Leadership	Listen to advice
VI – The Lovers	**VII – The Chariot**	**VIII – Strength**
Love	In charge	Confidence
Decisions	Determination	Good health
Romance	A visit/ trip	Balanced
A choice	Control	Discipline
Decide now	Focus on goal	Will power
Merging	Responsibility	Compassion

VIV – The Hermit	X – Wheel of Fortune	VI – Justice
Need Introspection Wisdom Awareness Meditation Teacher Direction	Change Luck A gamble Take a risk In motion Always moving	Balance required Right decision Harmony Effect End of conflict Good news in court
XII – The Hanged Man	XIII – Death	XIV – Temperance
Personal sacrifice No quick decisions Hang out and think Start planning Reversal Go within for answer	Transformation Changes needed Clean out things Let go of the old Rebirth / renewal Something's gone	Moderation Self-control Make adjustments Balancing Go slow Test things out
XV – The Devil	XVI – The Tower	XVII – The Star
Temptation Bad habits Vices Obsession Character flaws Greed	Major change Out of your control Accept and rebuild A "kick in the butt" Opposition Catastrophes	Hope Courage Dreams come true Optimistic Healthy body Reach for the stars

So You Wanna Read Tarot?

XVIII – The Moon	XIX – The Sun	XX – Judgement
Hidden things	Contentment	Valuable lessons
Deception	Success	Get your reward
Fears	Happiness	Realization
Illusion	Good luck	Awakening
Secrets	Optimism	Leap of faith
Enemies	Fulfillment	Liberation
XXI – The World		
Success		
Completion		
Overcome obstacles		
Reaching goals		
Realization		
Rewards earned		

CHEAT SHEET OF THE MINOR ARCANA - THE COURT CARDS (KEY WORDS)

King of Wands	Queen of Wands	Knight of Wands
Stubborn	Business Woman	Brings change
Noble	Leadership	Offering of a job
Hot-tempered	Nurturing person	Departure
Passionate	Inspires others	Willing to act
Manifests dreams	Domineering	Change in business
Page of Wands	**King of Cups**	**Queen of Cups**
Good news is coming	Family man	Nurtures emotions
The seeds of creativity	Generosity	Caregiver
Beginning communications	Has to balance emotions	Intuitive
New opportunities	Gives good advice	Tenderness
Young children	Mildness	Psychicness
Knight of Cups	**Page of Cups**	**King of Swords**
Offering of love	Start of emotions	Outspoken
Act upon dreams	Love letters	Knows right or wrong
Romance is coming	New relationships	Judge
Invitation	Devotion	Police
Proposal	Hearing news of love	Authority figure

Cheat Sheet Of The Numbered Cards
(Key Words)

Queen of Swords	Knight of Swords	Page of Swords
Fair and just	Action in defense	Begin action
Diplomatic	Misses the point	Begin defensiveness
Cuts things away	Aggressive	Need to communicate
Sets rules	Destructive	Start of conflict
Does on behalf of others	Fighter	Write something
King of Pentacles	**Queen of Pentacles**	**Knight of Pentacles**
Earthy person	Secure Woman	Bringing security
Security minded	Perfectionist	Offering a job
Banker, investor	Desire for Money	Promotion coming
Businessman	Being comfortable	Good luck with money
Stability	Having it all	A raise
Page of Pentacles		
Brings news – money		
News about a job		
Beginnings of security		
Feeling secure		
An Apprentice		

	Ace of Wands	**Two of Wands**
The Wands	Fresh Start Creativity/ passions New Beginnings Something new New Job	Making Plans You know what to do The right connections Turn ideas into reality You are responsible
Three of Wands	**Four of Wands**	**Five of Wands**
Accomplishments Your "ship is coming in" Success The time has come Making things happen	Celebration Harmony Joyous occasion Committed relationship A match made in heaven	Competition Struggle Need to overcome Don't give in A bit of turmoil
Six of Wands	**Seven of Wands**	**Eight of Wands**
Victory Success Reward time Completion Efforts are rewarded	Struggle to stay on top Overcome obstacles Tie up loose ends Take a stand Keep your position	Right on target! No delay Happening all at once Immediacy Progress is happening

Nine of Wands Fair and just Diplomatic Cuts things away Sets rules Does on behalf of others	**Ten of Wands** Carrying a heavy load Action in defense Misses the point Aggressive Stress	
The **Cups**	**Ace of Cups** Overflowing emotions Huge celebration New luck & happiness New love	**Two of Cups** Relationship start Initial encounter Romance Courtship
Three of Cups Fun with friends It's party-time! Happiness Celebrate with joy	**Four of Cups** What is offered? Lots of possibilities Don't overlook Be alert and aware	**Five of Cups** Disappointment Loss and regret Emotional upset Pick up the pieces

Six of Cups Old friendships Past acquaintances Old memories Childhood/ children	**Seven of Cups** Too many possibilities You are scattered Focus on one thing Need to organize	**Eight of Cups** Look for missing piece Make a plan Searching Leave the past behind
Ten of Cups Family happiness Secure life Everything is perfect Peacefulness	**The Swords**	**Ace of Swords** Fresh start in action Making things happen Victory is certain Strength & determination
Two of Swords In the Dark Need to decide Fork in the road Decide by yourself	**Three of Swords** Heartache Major disappointment Sorrow Heart is breaking	**Four of Swords** Rest & relaxation Take a break Go on vacation Recuperate

Five of Swords	Six of Swords	Seven of Swords
A no-win situation	Travel	Sneakiness
Defeat	Move away	Watch your back
At a stand-still	Take a different direction	Facing opposition
Sabotage	Time to move on	Trickery
Eight of Swords	**Nine of Swords**	**Ten of Swords**
Bound by thoughts	Worry and despair	Low point in life
Thinking too much	Causing worry	Worst is over
Sort out details	Don't panic	Have hope
Don't dwell on it	Have faith in self	Give up on lost cause
The Pentacles	**Ace of Pentacles**	**Two of Pentacles**
	Offer of success	Make a decision
	Money coming	Keep things in balance
	New financial start	Narrow your choices
	Positive rewards	You are juggling things

D. L. Cocchio

Three of Pentacles Further learning Counseling Skill Meeting	**Four of Pentacles** You cling to the familiar Can be selfish Need to share Don't be afraid of change	**Five of Pentacles** Temporary hardship Being ignored Money problems Difficult times
Six of Pentacles Unexpected money Much luck Help others Much success	**Seven of Pentacles** Look over what you have More growth Don't stop now Satisfaction	**Eight of Pentacles** Skilled Hard-working Perfection Reward for work
Nine of Pentacles Lots of prosperity Material possessions Excellent advice Inner peace	**Ten of Pentacles** Secure family Group prosperity Very comfortable Great home life	

Chapter 19 – Completion

If you are reading this final chapter, you have finished the book. You have, in essence, completed this entire course. You know all the tips and tricks in learning the Tarot. With practice and determination you will become a talented Tarot Reader. Don't feel embarrassed if you need to look up the cards or meanings. That is what the book is for - to be a handbook and to aid you in learning the cards. With practice, you will begin to rely on this book less and less, until one day you will not need it anymore. It's great to keep it as a reference, so keep it available on your bookshelf in case you need it in a pinch.

You should be proud of your accomplishment! You now will be able to read for yourself and your friends with confidence and poise. Bringing meaning and direction to someone's life is rewarding in itself.

I want to thank you for your dedication to learning the Tarot. Hopefully, you will begin to see yourself blossom and take charge of your life. Tarot allows us to see our paths clearer and make corrections if necessary. With the guidance of the cards, you will find many new doors of opportunity opening to you. Now it is up to you to grasp at the chances.

Happy Tarot Reading!

D.L. Cocchio

APPENDIX:
General Resources

Connolly, Eileen. Tarot. *A New Handbook for the Apprentice.* CA : Newcastle Publishing Co., Inc., 1990.

Garen, Nancy. *Tarot Made Easy.* New York : Fireside, Simon & Schuster, 1989.

Gray, Eden. *The Tarot Revealed.* New York: NAL Penguin, 1988.

McAdams, D. J. (2001). *The History of Tarot.* http://tarot-decks.com/tarotarticle.htm.

Ozaniec, Naomi. *The Illustrated Guide to Tarot.* New York : Sterling Publishing, 1999.

Salem Tarot (1998). *Tarot History.* http://www.tarothehermit.com/inforsheet.htm

Shadowwolf. (2001) *Tarot History.* http://roswell.fortunecity.com/leehigh/340/shadow/shadow5.html.

Tadfor-Little, T. (2000). *Tarot History.* Information Sheet. http://www.salemtarot.com/tarothistory.html.

Waite, Arthur Edward. *The Pictorial Key to the Tarot.* CT : U.S. Games Systems, Inc., 1994.

The author is hard at work
on her newest novel,

The Psychic Circle - Souls Entwined

*Book 1 in the
Psychic Circle Series*

a Young Adult
fiction novel
for teens
interested in
'the paranormal' world.

Visit D. L. Cocchio's website
to keep abreast of any news
on the release date.

www.dlcocchio.webs.com.

D. L. Cocchio

Other books by D. L. Cocchio...

Book 1 of the Amulet Series -
Be Careful What You Wish For

Best friends, Emily and Megan, are thrilled to find out that the amulet they bought at a Medieval Fair is supposed to make wishes come true. The magical amulet sends the girls on a fantastic journey back in time to 15th century England, where they encounter a host of unforgettable characters. Anne and her cousin, Richard, help the girls to try to uncover the truth about the amulet.

Will they find the answers they need to return to their own time? Can they avoid being caught? Join the girls and their new friends in this exciting adventure back in time.

Published by Magic Moon Press in 2011.
Paperback
ISBN-13: 978-1456555443
ISBN-10: 1-456555448

Available on the author's website: www.dlcocchio.webs.com.

also available at: www.amazon.com and www.createspace.com

Book 2 of the Amulet Series -
Magic By Moonlight

With a magical amulet in hand, three friends are whisked back in time to the Salem Witch Hunts, a terrible time in U.S. history. When Tituba, the Paris' slave, secretly teaches the children a lot more than housekeeping, like voodoo, fortune-telling, and spell casting, it leads to utter chaos in the village. Ultimately, Emily, Megan and Ben uncover a hidden secret which may alter the course of history.

Can they get the villagers to see what's really causing the fits and tantrums before they get accused of being witches themselves? Follow the friends on a fantastic adventure as they uncover a mystery when they travel back in time.

Published by Magic Moon Press in 2011.
Paperback & Ebook (Kindle/Nook)
ISBN-13: 9781-45375-861-8
ISBN-10: 1-45375-861-5

Available on the author's website: www.dlcocchio.webs.com.

also at: www.amazon.com, www.createspace.com, and www.smashwords.com (ebook)

D. L. Cocchio

INDEX

A

Arthur Waite, 11, 28
Arthurian Tarot, 13
Astrology, 1, 40, 43, 46, 49,
  53, 56, 59, 62, 65, 68, 71,
  75, 78, 81, 84, 87, 90, 93,
  96, 99, 102, 105, 117, 146,
  190

B

Bembo, 14, 27

C

Celtic Tarot, 13
Cheat Sheets, 189
Chinese Tarot, 15
Choose a deck, 10
Classic Tarot Decks, 11
Color Chart, 21
Court Cards, 113, 114, 115,
  118, 189, 194
Crowley, 12, 28
crystals, 20

D

Death, 12, 29, 33, 62, 80, 135,
  139, 188, 192

E

Egyptian Tarot Deck, 15

F

Fantasy Tarot Decks, 13

G

Games, 163
Gebelin, 27
Golden Dawn, 11, 12, 28, 29
gypsies, 26

H

Hanson-Roberts, 10, 11, 12
Herbal Tarot, 15
Historical Tarot Decks, 14

I

Incense Chart, 22
International Tarot Cards, 15

J

Japanese Tarot, 15
Jean-Baptiste Alliette, 27

K

Kabbalah, 27
Kaplan, 10, 11, 14, 15

L

Levi, 27
Lord of the Rings Tarot, 13

M

MacGregor, 12, 28
Major Arcana, 1, 25, 26, 32, 33, 34, 37, 111, 123, 134, 139, 165, 189, 191
Mathers, 12, 28
Medicine Woman Tarot, 13
Medieval Scapini Tarot, 14
Merlin Tarot, 13
Minor Arcana, 1, 25, 32, 35, 42, 123, 129, 189, 194
Morgan Greer Deck, 12

N

Norse Tarot, 15
Numbers, 124, 170, 180

O

origin, 25, 27, 29

P

Pamela Colman Smith, 11, 28
Paul Foster Case, 12, 29
Planets, 139

Q

Questions, 160

R

Rider-Waite, ii, 9, 11, 12, 31
Russian Tarot, 15

S

secret, 26, 27, 28, 47, 205
Spiritual Journey, 188
Spiritual Tarot Decks, 14
Spreads, 169
Stones, 21
Strength, 33, 64, 66, 134, 139, 188, 191, 198
Suits, 1, 108, 190
Swiss Tarot, 15

T

Tarot de Marseilles, 14
Tarot of the Cat People, 13
Tarot of the Old Path, 14
Tarot of the Sacred Rose, 14
Tarot of the Witches, 15
The Celtic Spread, 146
The Chariot, 33, 61, 139, 188, 191
The Emperor, 33, 52, 54, 139, 188, 191
The Empress, 33, 48, 50, 139, 188, 191
The Fool, 33, 34, 39, 41, 134, 139, 188, 191
The Hermit, 33, 67, 69, 139, 188, 192
The Hierophant, 33, 55, 57, 139, 188, 191
The High Priestess, 33, 45, 47, 50, 139, 191
The Lover's Tarot, 14
The Lovers, 33, 58, 139, 191
The Magician, 33, 42, 44, 50, 139, 188, 191

The Three Card Spread, 146, 147
The Tower, 33, 89, 139, 188, 192
The Wheel of Fortune, 33, 70, 139
Thoth Deck, 12
Timing, 110
Tree of Life, 27, 58

U

Universal Waite, 9, 11, 38

V

Visconzi-Sforza, 27

W

Wonderland Tarot, 13

Z

zodiac, 138
Zolar's Astrological Tarot, 12

FOLLOW YOUR DREAMS

www.ingramcontent.com/pod-product-compliance
Lightning Source LLC
Chambersburg PA
CBHW022356040426
42450CB00005B/214